THE GOOD LIFE
GETS BETTER

The Good Life Gets Better
1st Edition
August 2006

Published by Eye Books Ltd
8 Peacock Yard
London
SE17 3LH
Tel: +44 (0) 845 450 8870
website: www.eye-books.com

Set in Garamond and Frutiger
ISBN 10: 1903070481
ISBN 13: 9781903070482

British Library Cataloguing in Publication Data
A catalogue record for this book is available from the British Library

Printed and bound in Great Britain by Creative Print and Design

Cover image based upon photograph courtesy of Johnny Caribou, freelance writer and photographer, West Dawson City, who spends too much time at his neighbour Dorian's house.

Photographs on cover flaps courtesy of Dorian Amos and Pam Brown.

THE GOOD LIFE GETS BETTER

Dorian Amos

Published by Eye Books

To Bridget – the true sparkle in my life

ACKNOWLEDGEMENTS

First of all I would sincerely like to thank the many people who contacted me and gave their support after reading The Good Life; all their kind words have been most encouraging and treasured.

Thanks must go to Chris and Catriona at Eye Books for their support throughout the writing of this book and for putting up with it in its 'raw' format. Thanks also to Dan who continues to keep things happening despite all the communication difficulties with the hick in the northern bush.

I would also like to thank the writers about the North, past and present, Dick North and Pierre Burton to name a couple. Without their energy, discipline and commitment many of the fascinating stories of the North would be forgotten.

Dorian Amos
Yukon Territory

CONTENTS

INTRODUCTION

It's seven years since Bridget, my wife, and I decided that there has to be more to life than 'this'. I was a cartoonist and Bridget a psychiatric nurse, and we gave up everything we had ever worked for and immigrated to the Canadian wilderness for a bit of adventure. After making the decision to change our life, it took about five months to sell everything we owned before we said our goodbyes to friends and family and finally headed off into the endless dark woods of a different continent.

We were nervous but not scared, looking back; we were more naive than knowledgeable, but then, that is how it should be. We had little money, no legal right to be in Canada, no equipment, a short-legged dog called Boris and a rusty old Nissan truck. We also had enthusiasm and belief in what we were doing because we were tired of our mundane lives and really believed that there was more to life than what we had ... we just had to go and find it, whatever 'it' was.

I still remember the words of wisdom people gave us when they heard of our plans: 'You're too old to do that sort of thing, it's time you got a mortgage and settled down'; 'What are you going to do? You can't just build a place in paradise then sit in it for the rest of your life – you'll get bored!'; 'I'd love to just give up everything and swan off into the wilderness but I have responsibilities'; and my favorite – 'The grass is always greener...'. It's amazing how much free advice the chap who sits at the end of the bar can give you. If we had listened to all that advice we would have been scared, and our enthusiasm would have been diluted with other people's realities and fears. We had enough fears of our own; after all, you can't just give up your life and walk into the wilderness without a little anxiety. Where would we stay? Would we meet anyone out there? How big are the bears? What should we take? What would we do? The list of questions was endless and in the end we woke up and stopped asking them because in trying to answer them we were talking ourselves out of 'it'. We didn't care that the 'grass is always greener'. It is always bloody greener, always has been... always will be. That's why there's a stupid catchphrase about it. But what the stupid catchphrase does not address is why are you looking over the hedge in the first place? If you are thinking of better pasture it's because you have outgrown the one you're in, you are asking questions and are no longer following the herd, you actually want to leave for the greener grass and that was the difference between us and the chap at the end of the bar. We left... and found snow on it. It wasn't greener... it was different, as we knew it would be, because we dreamt of a golden land full of challenges, freedom and wilderness, we did not dream of greener grass. We found what we were looking for and we absolutely love it. As for getting bored, I'd try it, but we still have not had a chance to sit down. As for giving up our responsibilities, we did, easily, and found true ones... each other. And as for being too old to do this sort of thing and getting a mortgage... what a load of bollocks!

We left and felt free. We were unwashed and homeless for a year while we searched the backwoods for a place we could call home. And we finally found it after a canoe trip through 500 miles of wilderness into the far North. We found the Yukon. We found the City of Gold – Dawson City. We found the Klondike. And there we found the endless, remote wilderness. We built a cabin, struggled through -40°C winters, survived rotting ice, killed our meat, built our fires and gave birth to a son whom we named Jack.

And now, seven years on....

GOLD! GOLD! GOLD!

Sixty-Eight Rich Men on the Steamer *Portland*.
STACKS OF YELLOW METAL!

Seattle Post, 9:00 a.m. edition, July 17th, 1897

The Klondike Gold Rush began instantly and dramatically when the *Portland* sailed into Seattle harbour from St Michaels, Alaska, her hold full of the first gold out of Klondike and sixty-eight weather-beaten Yukon miners who were rich not only with gold but with life. Their arrival brought near hysteria to North America and Europe. Absolutely nothing in this world stirs quite so much emotion in the whole of humanity as GOLD. It has been the downfall of nations and the making of empires. It causes people to kill, steal and con, it makes some men sane and strips the sanity out of others. It has in the past, and to this day still does, lead ordinary men on wonderful, ridiculous adventures in far-off corners of the globe.

Living in the Klondike we hear many stories of these adventures. One is of Antoine from Dawson City, a true Yukoner through and through, tall, loud and crazy, living life at his pace and in his own direction, as free as the wind in the spruce in his exciting search for the Yukon's gold. And he found it, lots of it. The 'colours' he was finding were plentiful and full of riches and promise... but they killed him.

In the dark of winter and blinded by the glitter of gold, he cut a hole in the thick ice of the Yukon River downstream from Dawson and went diving 20 feet to the riverbed on the bend of the river. It was there that he found and collected the gold caught in the riffles of the ancient bedrock. The theory behind his expedition was reasonable for two factors. One, the Yukon River is so silty during the summer, due to hundreds of rivers and creeks draining into it, that it's impossible to see through the water, rendering it impossible to prospect. It is estimated that a dump-truck load of silt travels a fixed point every second during the height of the summer. In winter everything but the deepest water is frozen. Water levels drop and the river becomes clear.

Reason two, where Antoine was digging was downstream from the Klondike River in which billions of dollars of gold had been found. Naturally, huge amounts of gold are going to be washed into the Yukon River and get caught in the riffles of the bedrock at the first downstream bend.

It was a wonderful, inventive idea. But it was also crazy and ridiculous. Antoine was so blinded by gold fever that he totally overlooked one thing – the Yukon River... All went really well for about two weeks. He had been diving on a rope through a hole in the ice which was kept open by his mates sitting in a heated wall tent. Then one cold, windy day about an hour and a half before Antoine's air supply ran out his mates felt a tug on the rope to say he was surfacing. They gently coiled the rope as he came up from bedrock, then it went tight and all motion abruptly stopped. They waited anxiously. Minutes later three tugs of trouble jerked the line in their hands. His signal only told the poor fellows in the tent that he was in great danger. They waited and waited, the rope tight, the only sound the crackle of the wood stove. Antoine had become trapped in 10 feet of slush ice below the main ice. Time passed in the tent agonizingly slowly as his mates stared into the dark river, watching the line their friend was attached to twitch and shake, their cracked and weather-beaten hands gripping it tightly, waiting for the signal to pull, while all the time knowing that time was running out.

For Antoine we can only imagine the cold, the dark, the terror and the realism of his dilemma. He was stuck solid in a murky, cold world. The line around his waist led to safety and he must have felt his friends testing it with the occasional tug. His dark facemask was his world for his last cold hour.

The chaps in the tent, knowing Antoine's air supply was running out, in a final last-ditch attempt to save him pulled as hard as they could on the rope. It broke. Antoine was never seen again, his body never found, his riches never spent.

This is one of hundreds of stories that stud the history of man's search for gold and of the crazy, reckless and wonderful people who go beyond the last blue mountain in search of it. Antoine, I salute you.

Although not quite blinded, I feel the gold fever burning deep within me. It stirs wondrous thoughts of wealth, of adventure, of courage and adversity. In a place like the Yukon and the Klondike it is hard not to become infected with gold fever. This whole untamed land is all about gold and the wealth and hardships it creates. The lay of the land forces us to take certain routes through the mountains and valleys. These are natural passes and passageways, ancient ways through a rugged land with few roads or trails. Following them we are forced to walk in the footsteps of men and beasts and in the footsteps of history. The tough, rugged Klondikers of the gold rush, th e amazing athletes of the Han Nation, the Yukon wolf packs, the majestic bull moose, the awesome grizzly bear and the restless Barron Ground caribou have all walked these passes and passageways and their presence is worn into the rocks. While I travelled these unmarked routes through desolate wilderness something happened to me. I'm not sure what yet, but following a lone wolf track fills me with admiration. Finding a billycan hanging from a tree, the tree long since grown around it, fills me with awe. A lonely, rotten and forgotten wooden grave marker, split and weathered, still with the words 'a native of England' faintly visible, intrigues me, but it all represents adventure and adventure represents gold and gold is always on the other side of every mountain, in every valley, up every river, always on the other side. $28 billion worth of 'placer gold' has been taken from the Yukon since 1896. Placer gold means gold that has been weathered, broken and moved by ice and flood from a major source – the mystical, elusive Mother – and it is the elusive Mother Lode that haunts my dreams in the dark winter nights and it is the elusive Mother Lode I now intend to find.

WINTER 2003-4

December 2003

-40°C and the wind of change

It's mid December and the days are short, the sun conspicuous by its absence. A relentless cold presses down from clear skies. Everything is motionless, engulfed in a white, frozen silence, and not a whisper of wind stirs the snow-clad spruce which bow to the awesome power of the Yukon winter. Dusk is creeping out of the forest by 2.30 in the afternoon. Stalking it is the sinister chill of the night that parades sparkling constellations and whirling northern lights in a dark, domed sky until the twilight of dawn dilutes the display just before 10 in the morning. Below our cabin thick white ice fog hangs in the snaking river valley shrouding islands and ice as if they didn't exist. It's been like this for what seems like weeks now but they say on the radio it's finally going to warm up tomorrow. That actually means it might be -25°C instead of -48°C, which is incredibly warm after a week of 'get the dog in' weather. At -25°C we can quite happily go about our daily lives with only a few minor adjustments such as putting on a hat, not having to think about not putting anything on the floor of the cabin in case it freezes, and putting an extra log in the stove. But at -40°C or lower, life becomes extraordinary.

I find living in -40°C temperatures staggeringly difficult because nothing is designed for it, not even ice. Twelve-feet-thick river ice can crack and split causing previously-frozen rivers to open! Strange things happen, trees suddenly split apart with a massive crack that echoes for miles in the silent forest, Boris craps under the cabin and smoke from the wood-stove doesn't actually rise but lingers on the porch like the Avon Lady desperately searching for a doorbell.

I am definitely not designed for weather this cold. I'm forever picking ice from my nose, while my ears blister, cheeks go white, eyelids freeze shut and facial hair becomes a breeding ground for icicles and other festive, winter, fluffy bits. But what I find most staggering of all is the fact that every time it's -40°C, we always have to go to town.

The process of going to town as a family is a long and painful one because it takes careful planning, and planning we have always had difficulty with; but now it is almost impossible with a hyper two-year-old Spiderman who shoots everything that moves with anything that's handy.

We haven't been to town for two months, and now that the Yukon River is frozen which makes a trip to town possible, the call for fresh fruit and veg is overwhelming, so tomorrow we've decided to take the truck, because if we don't, we won't stand a chance of getting anything remotely carrot-like back to the cabin without it freezing. It's going to be interesting. This cold spell looks like it's staying – let's hope the weatherman's right for a change.

The weatherman's wrong as usual. I opened the door of the cabin this morning and was engulfed in a veil of steam from the dark. Opening the door of the cabin every morning is our way of forecasting the day. The amount of steam that erupts when the cold air meets the cabin air is proportionate to the temperature – the colder it is the more steam there is; and the temperature is proportionate to the success of the day – the colder it is means the chance of success decreases.

It's probably about 10.30 a.m., daylight is creeping over the spruce trees and a raven is gurgling from somewhere aloft. More ice has built up on the windows overnight and Boris is refusing to move from the front of the wood-stove as Bridge battles to put another log on. I sit at the window with a mug of tea and watch the daylight gradually bring a foreboding sparkle to the snow while I pluck up the courage to go outside and find the truck.

When I find the truck and eventually dig it out from under a winter's supply of snow, the sun is just cresting the trees, which is as high as it gets this time of year, but it has no heat in it. We haven't used the truck since sometime in October so of course it won't start. At this temperature of -41°C, the oil in the engine is so hard the pistons struggle to move through it, the seats, tyres and suspension are all solid, and just turning the stiff key causes the battery to die quicker than a West-Country hedgehog on the A303.

I dig a hole in the snow just in front of the truck, put a sheet metal stove in it and extend the chimney up under the truck's engine. After taking the battery and spark plugs into the cabin to warm up, I light a fire in the stove and dash back to the cabin to wait. As the short daylight hours pass I watch the smoke from the sheet metal stove rise around the bonnet of the truck melting all the unnecessary plastic bits and forever changing the smell of the truck from stale peanut butter sandwiches to a dirty smoke house.

Using these handy tips, we have in the past spent three entire days trying to turn the truck from a red garden ornament into an automobile that is automated. Spurred on by the thought of ten-day-old lettuce, failure on the first day has only hardened our resolve. The next day sees the same struggle except I usually throw in a couple of nifty, kung-fu-style chops to the bonnet. Finally, with no change except having drained the battery, I put some moose sandwiches, a battery charger and the dead battery in a backpack and walk into town, hoping the battery won't freeze before I can charge it in the nearest electrical socket so I can try again the next day.

This time, however, it seems we might be lucky. After a couple of hours of warming the truck with the sheet metal stove, I reconnect the warmed battery and spark plugs. It takes both hands to turn the frozen key stem, but when I do the truck reluctantly coughs into life for a few brief but encouraging moments, then dies. I wait a couple of freezing seconds then turn the key again. This time it bursts into life with a roar, and rattles and shakes as an enormous amount of blue smoke bellows out of the exhaust. I keep the throttle to the floor knowing I'm doing un-repairable damage and watch the snow vibrate and crack on the windscreen and steam from the frosted engine mix with the blue smoke as the engine begins to warm. After about ten minutes of sitting on the frozen seat, the cold seeping through every garment I'm wearing, I pluck up the courage to take my foot off the accelerator and the truck idles, not well, but it idles. SUCCESS! Crispy carrots here we come!

While we let the truck warm up for an hour, Bridge and I go through the yearly ritual of finding the wallet, because we always forget where we left it the October before. After we locate it, we load Boris, Little Jack a.k.a. Spiderman, survival kits, chainsaw, food and laundry into the truck knowing that our real troubles are about to start. With a few revs and a sudden release of the clutch, we un-stick the tyres and drive through the snow to the river. The tyres are frozen square and half the truck is only doing half of what it should be doing, while we freeze on frozen seats inside the cab and frost up the windows. As we drive we don't so much sing *Chitty Chitty Bang Bang* in a fun family way but simply pray nothing snaps and leaves us stranded.

On the river the fog is thick and swirling in a strong Alaskan wind. As we approach we see a track already across the ice, and water running over the shore ice like a steaming lava flow because the river has cracked somewhere up river. Bridge and Little Jack stay in the truck to keep it running as I walk out on to the jumble of ice which is creaking and cracking in the cold air. With the chainsaw I cut into the ice until the two-feet bar is buried vertically. No water spews out, which means the ice is thicker than two feet. I wave to Bridge who drives the truck slowly on to the ice while I test another spot with the saw. The wind coming out of the north is gnawing at my face, freezing it within seconds. I'm bundled up in everything I own without a hint of skin exposed, but my right temple feels like someone is driving a nail into it.

I look back at the truck, bright red and steaming in a totally white, fog-blurred world and I wonder how Bridge is feeling driving on to the ice – the first time is always nerve racking, especially when you can't see properly through the frosted windows. I cut into the ice once more and still no water comes out. My fingers holding the saw are now virtually numb. The ice seems safe enough so I run back to the truck to escape the wind. Bridge drives over the jumbled ice, and with every bump we pray for solid ground as we are thrown backwards and forwards in our frozen hard seats. The heater whines in its struggle to pump cold air, the windscreen creeks then cracks and Little Jack shoots Boris with a paint roller... there must be something seriously addictive about fresh lettuce.

In town the snow is dirty. Wood smoke mingles with truck exhaust and ice fog hangs low like smog in the street. Nobody's around, but the lights are on in the houses, and the shops on Front Street shine with tacky Christmas decorations and pipe out carols to no-one in the -40°C wind.

We go for lunch and stock up on supplies, and the longer we're in town the more people we encounter. It's nice to chat and catch up on what's been happening in the world after our two months of solitude across the river, but we begin to notice an unusual buzz around town and it doesn't take us long to discover the reason. The Government has announced the building of the Yukon River Bridge. Our hearts sink into the snow. They are going to build a massive steel bridge across the river to join Dawson to nowhere. A bridge will really affect our lives. There will be no more lonely Freeze Ups, no more struggling to cross the river at Break Up. The town will expand around us and electricity poles will march up the hill in a regimented line through unkempt natural beauty. Since we arrived in the Yukon over seven years ago everyone has been talking about a bridge. Several people have moved across the river and built cabins in the trees to secure land in the hope of making a quick buck. I now know why last September an odd chap from the phone company, wearing bright orange overalls and a thick fur hat, was struggling through the woods with a GPS.

It truly is a shame. The town has so much charm, history and character which will be overshadowed by a huge, modern, steel bridge. Dawson City is a real frontier town, a gold rush town built on gold and dreams, and a bridge will turn it into a typical North American highway town. At the moment Dawson is the end of the road and attracts 'The Colorful Five Percent', the people who can't, won't or refuse to fit into the plastic, shiny world outside where cholesterol levels, the price of petrol and the latest style of jeans depict the way people live, instead of the day length, the mercury level in the thermometer and the rutting season of large leggy ungulates.

Dawson City has gone through monumental changes in its short but dynamic history. Before 1896 it didn't exist, the area being a frozen swamp used by the Han Nation as a fishing camp. Besides the Han Nation and other First Nation bands the whole territory held only a few hundred brave prospectors or Sourdoughs, so-called because they carried in a bag on their belts a fermenting yeast, sugar and flour mix which they used as a starter for making sourdough bread. They lived a hard but quiet life governed by an honorable code and the Yukon's weather as they sought hidden fortunes in unknown, nameless creeks. Then on 17 August 1896 George Carmack stumbled upon unimaginable wealth lying in the bottom of Rabbit Creek (later renamed Bonanza Creek) and the frozen swamp began to fill up with tatty canvas tents and the odd hastily-built cabin as word of the discovery drifted throughout the Yukon. Men dragged their outfits to the frozen swamp from the established mining camps of Circle City, Alaska, and Forty Mile, Yukon, just for a chance at the rumoured gold lying by the ton beneath the frozen muskeg. Very quickly, tented saloons and rough lumber dance halls began to appear as outsiders who had heard the whispers and climbed the passes arrived to make their fortunes. By the summer of 1897, a year later, 3,500 people were crammed onto the frozen swampland, and gold nuggets were thrown around like toffees in a parade. The hillsides were stripped of trees, and roughly-constructed cabins, hotels, casinos and saloons were built in their place, the streets turned to mud and the honorable way of the Yukon order of Sourdoughs counted for nothing. They felt out of place and vulnerable in the rapidly growing town where gambling, drinking and dance hall girls came before honour, respect and honesty. Many moved on, knowing things were only going to get worse, because news of the strike had not yet reached the

South. When it did, hundreds of thousands would burn with a fever which would compel them to climb the passes and run the rapids until they too reached the end of the rainbow, bringing with them change.

Creating change this time, however, seems to be the aim of a small, rather loud percentage of the town that has forgotten why they moved to the Yukon. They have become stuck trying to make a conventional living in a remote, small, northern town with dirt streets, no real services and no sun for a month in January. They are too busy complaining about the cost of freight to get out into the raw, natural beauty which surrounds them for thousands of miles. All they see is what they haven't got – paved roads, proper sewers, dependable electricity, a Kentucky Fried Chicken drive-through, and a bridge, and it's not fair because everywhere else in Canada has. They are too busy trying to make money selling dingy hotel rooms and failing to see what they do have, which is beauty and wonder all around them, the chance to sit, alone, in the endless, snow-choked forest by a fire and listen to the silence, the chance to hunt their own meat and to drift for miles on untamed remote rivers snaking through unimaginable country, and the irony is nowhere else can offer that. Instead, the small, rather loud few want the chance to make a name for themselves and a lot of money by bringing Dawson City into the modern world, making it like everywhere else, for the greater good of us all but especially themselves.

We have come to the far North and built a home out in the bush because of what it offers, because of what is here and because it is not like everywhere else. It enables us to live a life full of challenges, a life we can look back on and be proud of, that we live and feel every day, but all that is now threatened because some business owners in town need a bridge to make more money. We feel a strange kin with the Sourdoughs. They were independent men who enjoyed the struggle of poling alone up a wild, unmapped river, while ice built up around their boat and the nip in the air stung their faces, their main thought being the gold that had to lie in the bottom of a creek around the next bend. They pushed all boundaries and lived life on the edge. They were the select few who ventured far into the dark forest of the northern spruce, they needed the unknown and the thrill of discovering what lay over the next mountain. It was only when they found what they were supposedly looking for, i.e. gold (the only legitimate reason a sane man wanders through wilderness with purpose), that things changed. As soon as gold was struck anywhere in the North, word spread like chicken pox at daycare. Thugs, gamblers, priests, prostitutes, dance hall girls and police flocked to the previously unknown area to make money, build bridges, save savages and make names for themselves.

Dawson City is a testament to this. As churches, cabins and casinos sprang up and the area became 'civilized', the lonely prospector found himself surrounded by what he had escaped from. All of a sudden he was subject to other men's laws and religion. He had to take his hat off to eat, bow and kneel on Sundays, he was robbed and conned and made into a criminal if he carried a gun. When the noise of plunking pianos, drunken brawls and fighting dogs became impossible to bear, he left once more to wander the lonely misty valleys in search of what he was supposedly looking for.

After a bumpy ride home during which we sank into silence, we reach our cabin in the dark. It is our home, built with our own hands, and it has sheltered us from the ravages of the Yukon's storms for over five years. It stands silently in the spruce, silhouetted by a clear sky studded with brilliant stars and a distant moon, but as we walk up to the door all we see hanging over it is the dark cloud which no wind can clear.

January 2004

Cabin-bound and fighting the fever

With my job as a Park Ranger comes a Ranger cabin in the Tombstone Mountains. It is eight feet by twelve, which gives me no room to do Yoga if I ever felt like it, but it's a great little cabin, with a wood-stove, a small table and a bed. I use it as a base for week-long winter patrols in the mountains, and it makes life a little more comfortable at the end of each day. However, I'd just been cabin bound in it for six days and it got progressively smaller! A vicious wind raged constantly, driving the -50°C air under the door like a rising tide. The clear nights went on forever as I huddled in the dim light of the wood-stove, longing to get out under the sparkling constellations domed over the sky, but when I did venture out I lasted minutes, and was amazed to see icicles down the side of the cabin chimney while smoke billowed from the stack. The snow was drifting all around the cabin so I had to walk everywhere in snowshoes while the wind sucked the heat from my body. Many a time, after a quick jaunt outside, I made it back to the cabin and found the door blown open and the place full of snow, freezing by the minute.

It's times like that, when I'm isolated and Bridge and Little Jack are miles away at home in the cabin across the river and I'm stuck, imprisoned in a tiny log cabin by a brutal storm, that my mind races with wonder and questions about what the heck we are doing and where the heck we are going. Adventure for adventure's sake seems to be dulled now that Little Jack is running around happy and contented and oblivious to the fact there are things like computer games and Garfield in this world. We need a reason, a legitimate reason, for relishing these hardships, for sailing close to the wind, not knowing if we'll get home by nightfall or what the next day will bring. We really do need a realistic reason for it all. Maybe we are being selfish, even foolish, maybe we should go back and get a mortgage on a house that has running water and a lawn and where the dustmen come and take the rubbish away on Wednesdays. I could get a steady job as a bus driver, barman or cartoonist again. Jack could have friends and go to school in a white shirt, grey shorts and polished Clark's shoes. Bridge could put away the chainsaw and join a club, go for coffee at a friend's house or get a part-time job at the library. Sometimes the thought of those things seems fantastic! I could even go for a pint of bitter in the Chicken and Chaplin after a hard day's work, see the chaps, tell rude jokes and moan about the price of parking meters. I miss, even long for, all those things sometimes. England has its unique quirks and will forever be with me. British Rail serving warm cans of lager but running late, absolutely no free parking, and the old git at the end of the oak bar in every pub who knows it's going to be a harsh winter because of the number of blackberries in the hedges are all truly British and I miss them greatly, but something keeps me here in the wild North Land. Something here promises the unknown, promises excitement and adventure, and I now believe it to be the challenge of finding the elusive Mother Lode lying in the frozen mud, ready to create a world-wide storm.

For a long time now we have drifted through the mountains and along the rivers of the Yukon and I have felt the tug, asked the question, and dreamed the dream of gold in the creek bed around the next bend. The problem is, I've always been a logical person and I think there is absolutely nothing logical about prospecting for gold. It takes a dreamer to search thousands upon thousands of miles of pristine wilderness for the chance of finding a fortune, but people do. But no matter how you look at it, the Mother Lode itself is a logical concept. Only forty per cent of the supposed gold hidden in the Yukon's wilderness has been mined and that gold is placer gold. It has been peeled by the forces of nature like a man whittling a stick; it came from somewhere, somewhere big, the Mother Lode. The Yukon is eight times bigger than England and has not been explored properly on the ground. There are still hundreds of thousands of acres that have not felt the tread of a human foot. There are hundreds, if not thousands, of unnamed creeks that have still not felt the bite of a shovel or the steel of a gold pan, and unfortunately for Bridge and Little Jack I have read somewhere that only 0.000002 per cent of one per cent of the total estimated gold in the earth has been recovered.

When I'm stuck for six days in a small draughty cabin, running out of food and struggling to stay sane, the adventure of gold is what fills my thoughts and takes them over the last blue mountain into the unknown, and that is what keeps me here.

February 2004

Just another -40°C day

The day is clear, cold and classic -40°C. It doesn't feel as cold as it is because the sun is shining, but the two ravens with frost around their faces, huddled together atop a frosted alder tree, look cold. Our cabin is just high enough on the hill to look over the ice fog hanging in the river valley so we can see forever into the brittle, clear day right to the mountains on the horizon. All movement is halted and all sound engulfed by the cold that rains down on this white land from the flawless sky.

We are running out of firewood and I intended to go looking for dead standing trees on the skidoo today but I can't get it going. It amazes me every time how really cold metal gets at -40°C. The skidoo is frozen, totally seized with cold. If I touch any metal on it with bare hands I freeze to it; even with gloves on, the cold in the metal soaks the glove like a liquid freezing the hands. I put a couple of lit candles against the engine earlier and threw a tarpaulin over the bonnet to try and warm it up a little so I could at least pull out the starter cord. If I'm careful and gentle I can pull it out now, but it takes forever to retract back into the engine block and doesn't seem to create anything remotely close to a spark.

I open the bonnet as one of the ravens gurgles in the quiet. Maybe it's telling me something and maybe I should listen, because those two old timers in that tree have been in this brutal land for probably fifty years (they live for nearly eighty years). I acknowledge them with a whistle which seems to go unnoticed, then I try to take off one of the spark plug leads, but it's too brittle and snaps. It's at times like this that I wish I'd got the wood in the fall, back then when life was easy. Undaunted, I reach for the tool kit under the seat and go into the cabin for a cup of tea and wait for the tools to warm up to a useable temperature.

Full of tea and warmth I put on my heavy winter gear again, pull my facemask up over my face and venture out to accomplish my mission. The spark plugs are stiff but I manage to undo them with my briefly steaming, adjustable wrench fresh from the top of the wood-stove. To get the skidoo going in these temperatures it needs all the help it can get, so my plan is to pour a little petrol into each cylinder, put the plugs back in and pull the cord... it will then start. It will. It must! I put the plugs on the wood-stove while I look for the petrol can. I find it empty and half buried under a pile of snow, one corner of which is stained yellow, so I cuss Boris as I dig it out. I need to fill it by siphoning some petrol out of the 45-gallon barrel that stands waist high in snow near the outhouse. I hesitate, looking at the wood pile to see if all this is really necessary; it is. I find the siphon hose hanging on its rusty nail by the shed and I gently pick it off, trying not to twist or bend it in case it snaps, and carry it into the cabin to warm up.

After another cup of tea I put on all my winter gear again and trudge back to the barrel of petrol with the now briefly flexible siphon hose. Knowing it's only a matter of minutes before I won't be able to bend it, I hastily put one end into the barrel, crouch in the snow next to the jerry can, put the other end into my mouth and suck. As the ravens watch me gurgle, I see the petrol in the hose rise out of the drum, over the arc in the hose and down into my mouth. Instantly I feel as if I've been hit in the teeth with a hammer and am felled. I am almost puking with the pain in my mouth from the -40°C petrol against my teeth. That was not the plan. I wanted to avoid getting it in my mouth but it was too quick. I really think it has cracked my teeth as I spit and cough like a ten-year-old tasting tequila. As the pain arcs to my forehead I stagger to my feet to grab the hose and stem the flow of petrol soaking into my coat. It snaps and the flow slows to a drip. I am now unbelievably cold and burping up petrol fumes that make me want to vomit. My teeth feel as if they are in pieces and falling out of my mouth, and to top it off the ravens on the alder are gurgling to each other, almost laughing, so I give up and stagger into the cabin to collapse by the stove. With the hose snapped we can't get the petrol out of the barrel. I think it's going to be one of those days where we just sit in front of the stove and drink tea. If we run out of firewood before this cold snap ends we'll have to use the sofa.

A light wind was blowing this morning and it seemed to be warming things up a little. The temperature when I went out first thing was -37°C which is a few degrees warmer than yesterday. The wind was just rocking the snow-laden spruce slightly and dislodging some of the snow from the upper branches. As the morning progressed the wind got stronger and stronger and the temperature climbed. Now it's mid-afternoon and wind is slamming into the cabin with tremendous gusts. The poor spruce are bending and swaying, some are snapping, snow on the ground is being whipped up and flown back into the sky. But the most staggering thing is that the temperature is now 2°C. It's incredible. Within hours the cold has been blown out of the valley and the temperature has risen more than 40°. It is so warm. There is no snow left on the trees so they look green again and are standing tall. The wind is really punishing them – one second they are upright, the next they are bent to 30°. The windows in the cabin actually creek when a gust comes and we wait nervously for the breaking of glass until it subsides. For a land that was, moments ago, so still, white and frozen, the contrast is amazing. Movement and noise are everywhere. Colour has instantly returned since the snow has blown from the trees. Snow drifts are crawling across the ground and burying anything in their path. This wind is what is known as a Chinook – a warm channel of air blowing in from the South. We get them occasionally during the winter but I have never seen one so violent and with such drastic results.

The wind lasts for probably fourteen hours and in that time we wait for disaster as huge trees around us snap and fall, but it doesn't come. After the wind has gone, the valley falls quiet again and movement stops. It is so warm, 5°C, and it takes a good twenty-four hours before the temperature drops to -20°C. Hindsight is a wonderful thing but I wish I'd tried to start the skidoo today.

The storm

February 2004

Bridge has 'the look': she has just returned from town where she learnt that the new bridge is going to be 40 feet high and is being built so development can spread around us. After seventeen years, I know the look and I know a storm is brewing so I throw some wood on the stove and hunker down.

It's a surprisingly rapid storm but a powerful one, and although windswept, I have survived it, for the politicians got the full force of the blast. Bridge was half way through making the tea when she burst into what can only be described as an interesting rant. It appears we have to move and move today. 'We can't live under the threat of pooper scoopers, road signs, Wal-Mart with all its third-world-exploited plastic crap, false smiles, and pristine, white-tiled bathrooms. It is all coming, coming across the river into our trees.' The storm lasted for a brief but ferocious four minutes and I envied Boris as he slinked out of the cabin for the safety of the woodpile. 'We have to go deeper into the bush, away from bigots and bullshit.' Bridge had something to say and she was saying it. She stomped around the cabin with eyebrows levelled, thumping her fist on any vertical surface as the veins in her temples swelled to resemble the path of the M3 on a cheap road map. I sat staring into the fire, nodding my head at the right moments and tutting whenever politicians' names were mentioned. She did, however, have a point. We don't want a bridge or neighbours, and we definitely do not want electricity or phones which the bridge will bring. And I believe it is true that just because it's difficult to sell pizzas, a round of golf or Corel Draw in any quantity in Dawson City, a $35 million bridge is to be built so that 'hopefully' tourists will come and stale pizza will sell like the 308 bullets, large bags of flour and dog sled runners have done for years.

After the storm Bridge flops down next to me on the tatty sofa and nurses her bruised fist. I wait a respectful few minutes then cautiously mention the tug that the mysterious gold has on my sanity. I am careful with my words at first, but within moments my excitement unleashes them and casts them into the air like an aria. I float on a glorious, golden, verbal cascade for three wonderful minutes, lost in the freedom and romance of the mysterious North. When the words suddenly dry up and I feel stupid, I sit down sheepishly. Although Bridge is looking at me worriedly, a broad smile lightens her delightfully pretty face and I know I am going to have to wait a couple of years for a pint of bitter at the Chicken and Chaplin because adventure is coming, and it rumbles freely behind the mountains like an impending thunderstorm.

The pressure of the bridge, future development and the coming of utilities are going to make us move further into the wilderness. We have to move because we love the fact that we sit in peace on the deck in the sun and know that what sounded like the phone ringing in the cabin is most definitely not the phone ringing in the cabin. We love the fact we don't need security chains, curtains or keys, deadbolts or spy holes on the door. We love the fact our personal space is not invaded every morning because we have to squeeze onto a tube train full of grumpy commuters wondering what has happened to their youth. In short, we love our chosen bumpy path.

With the decision made to go beyond the last blue mountain with a purpose, not just for adventure, our life in this harsh northern land seems to have meaning. It has become legitimate, we aren't floating on a frozen wind hoping for challenges then praying for them to stop. We've already been there and done that by coming north to the Yukon and meeting her blindly like groveling servants before a queen. We have toiled with her, challenging her for challenge's sake, and she has made us run, crawl, cry, and go hungry. But during the past seven years we have learnt a great deal from her and now feel ready to go deeper into her golden heart. We know her many moods because we've survived them.

Knowing we have something in common with the adventurous prospectors who entered this remote land when no map displayed her secrets, the threat to our way of life seems a little easier to handle. We wished we could have been there with them, when the Han Nation, fit and strong on the Yukon's bounty and unhindered by roads, followed the caribou and salmon, but that time is gone. It is time for the future, and our concern and disappointment shrivels in comparison to the future that lies before us in the vast North Land where anything can happen and a fortune in gold lies hidden in one of its nameless creeks.

SPRING 2004

April 2004

Mountain magic

The sun is hitting the mountains around us earlier and earlier each day. As Bridge and I sit in the snow sipping our morning tea we soak up the silence. The only sounds to waft into the stunning mountain vista around us are the faint chattering of ptarmigan further up the valley and the occasional crackle of the wood-stove in the wall tent keeping Little Jack warm as he sleeps. We are watching the snow-covered mountain in front of us turn a pastel shade of pink at its jagged summit, and minute by minute the pink bleeds down the pale blue slopes pushing back the shadows of the valley until the sun crests the mountains behind and bathes the valley in glorious sunshine. We look at each other and smile as if we have just watched the end of a classic play at the theatre.

It's mid-April and we have come into the mountains to wait out the break-up of the Yukon River. After I went through the ice and nearly drowned a couple of years ago, we take little chances with the river. We usually hole up in the cabin and wait until the ice is gone, but this year we have come and set up a base camp to get an early start on searching the maze of hidden valleys around us in the hope that one might show signs that could reveal gold when the snow is gone.

It's another brilliant Yukon day. The sky is clear and pure blue, the April sun is now high in the sky reflecting off the endless carpet of mountain snow and chasing away the last of the -20°C night air. I am skiing up a valley east of camp to see what lies over the ridge. When I say skiing, I actually mean straining muscles I didn't know existed, bum-surfing down hills and continually crashing into the snow with all the flair of Eddy the Eagle with no specs. The problem is not so much the crashing as the getting up again. The snow is four to six feet thick, and getting vertical after a rather dramatic nose dive presents a multitude of challenges. I can't use my arms because they just aren't long enough to touch a solid base, and by trying I make the situation a whole lot worse and end up much more horizontal than necessary. I try with my ski poles but they are only five feet long, so everything starts promisingly enough and I can get to a low squat, then I run out of lift and my skies take off downhill and I'm back to writhing around in the snow. I'm beginning to think this cross country skiing lark was a complete wind-up by the cocky little self-confessed snow-boarder I bought my skies from at the Whitehorse sports store. As I recall, I was a bit suspicious about his so-called expertise when he kept calling me 'Dude' and saying 'Whoah!' (with eyebrow movements that were too highly exaggerated to be normal) after everything I said.

Cross country skiing, I thought, was going to be the answer to our problem of getting into remote valleys early. I have seen a couple of people doing it around town and it looks easy enough but this is turning into a nightmare.

When I finally get upright I think the skis are going to snap as I sink in the middle and both ends curl upwards in the soft snow. Maybe I'm doing it wrong, or my pack is too heavy – I don't have a clue. Sometimes I wish we could take lessons on this stuff, but really, how hard can it be? There are no moving parts and no license is required. I am, however, beginning to think there should be a health warning on the packet, perhaps a picture of a hapless chap in sporty-looking ski wear with two broken legs and 'WARNING! Skiing stunts your morale' printed below. Something should have clicked when I saw Bridge testing her new skis. She was at the top of a precipitous slope – I'll be fair, it had a grade of one inch to fifteen feet – her bum was in the air, and her arms stretched out in front grasping the vertical ski poles as if she was in the countdown to the start of the women's final downhill ski race at the Olympics. After considerable shuffling forward and much bum wriggling, her weight shifted and she started down the slope at warp factor slow. This movement was followed a split second later by a sudden upright stance and straight arm circular wave as if she had suddenly seen a loved one at a third-world airport.

After this imaginative but desperate attempt at control, she ground to a halt and fell over backwards vowing never to strap anything five feet long to her feet again.

April 2004

Racing wolves

After continually failing on cross country skis, I have decided to walk up the valley on snowshoes. The conditions are obviously not right for skiing! We are far too remote out here to risk injury, and besides, I am not feeling anatomically correct after straining a few extra never-before-known muscles that have been lurking all this time in peculiar parts of my body. The walking is tough and slow going, but if I stay on the wind-blown bluffs the snow is not as deep as it is in the valley.

By mid-morning a snow storm starts. One minute I can see the thin wisp of smoke coming from our camp in the spruce below, the next I can't see two feet in front of me. The wind is bitter and has come from nowhere, bringing with it the haunting howls of wolves somewhere in the distance to my left.

I find relative shelter below a snowdrift which stands out from the top of a bluff like a frozen rip curl arching into the valley below. I have with me an amazing invention and a must for all adventurous prospectors. It's a Kelly Kettle and it truly is a life saver. It boils water in minutes and runs on twigs, leaves or shavings so you don't have to carry heavy fuel canisters. I just stuff snow in the chamber, light a small fire out of whatever I can find and within minutes have warm hands and boiling water for soup.

Judging by their howls the wolves are in this valley and moving quickly. Although I can't see them through the whiteout I think there are about six of them spread out above me. If they continue on their present course, they will be going right past camp which could be a problem for Boris because wolves entice dogs out into the woods and eat them. I know that sounds like a fairy tale, or the sort of thing you tell your dog to keep him in the garden, but it really happens. Our neighbour Brent lost a couple of dogs to wolves right off their chains in his dog yard last winter. I decide to head back down and tie Boris up; he's not the most intelligent animal and he might think the wolves passing is a chance for a smoke behind the bike sheds with the big boys from Year Five.

It's easier going down than coming up but my trail has already blown in. I still cannot see a thing and nearly go off the end of a bluff, so I slow down a bit. The wolves are getting closer, their lonesome wails carrying far on this wind, so they are probably a couple of miles away now which is a little bit daunting because they were probably four miles away only minutes ago.

My descent turns into a race. The wolves are right behind me howling to each other as they hug the valley depths. I still cannot see them, but then I can't see much except swirling snow. I bet not many people can say they've raced a wolf pack down a mountain – it's actually quite exciting. As I near the lower slopes and the spindly tree-line I pray my trail in the trees will be more sheltered from the wind and will not have blown in so that I can make better progress.

When I enter the woods, only the wind in the trees is howling; the wolves seem to have gone. Maybe they reached my lunch spot, caught wind of me and turned back. At camp, Bridge and Jack are inside the battened-down tent, huddled by the wood-stove and reading *Fat Charlie's Circus*. Boris is nowhere to be seen. We call for him, our calls taken quickly by the wind, but he eventually comes out from beneath a big spruce as if to say, 'I'm sleeping here, so this better be important!' It's then that we hear the wolves again, this time very close. They are in the trees around camp. Holding Boris tightly we stand together in silence outside the tent and listen excitedly to the wonder and mysteriousness of the unseen wolf pack passing camp. I look at two-year-old Little Jack.

Snow is blowing around his weather-tanned face. The wind is reddening his cheeks and watering his eyes. But those eyes are alive with excitement and discovery as he awaits, with finger to his ear, the next howl of the wolf.

After lingering for a moment near the camp, the wolves, hidden by the veil of spruce and swirling snow, continue past and we listen until they are way down the valley before we release Boris to strut, grunt and growl.

The next day I finally make it to the top of the valley east of camp and sit on a wind-swept ridge, totally exhausted. It's a glorious bright day with not a breath of wind and I now know what's on the other side of this valley – more mountains and more valleys all brilliant white and shining, stretching out like an endless, white, jagged spruce forest beneath the clear blue sky. It's a spectacular site.

This perfect wilderness scene is a little bit overwhelming. We have travelled 50 miles from our cabin outside Dawson City to make our base camp and it has taken me the better part of a week to climb to the top of this one short valley just to see what is on the other side. It's hard to imagine the resolve of the old prospectors trudging through these mountain passes, alone and battling the notorious Yukon elements with little more than a shovel, a gold pan, a side of bacon and a couple of pounds of flour and beans on their backs. In their pockets they kept the most important things – dry matches, sourdough starter and their precious ever-empty but optimistic gold poke.

Looking at the scene before me I can understand why, in a hundred years of intense mining, only forty per cent of the Yukon's gold has been excavated, for there is not a visible road in this view for hundreds of miles, and I'm facing south!

When the thin mountain air chills my body I walk along the ridgeline, marvelling at those prospectors who entered this area in the early nineteenth century. It was a white patch on the map, an unknown wasteland, stretching across the top of Canada from coast to coast and reaching as far south as Slave Lake, Alberta. The courage it must have taken to wander completely alone into this expanse is incredible. To get where

I am standing would have taken years not days. Today I can look at maps and access the general area via the infamous Dempster Highway and think it's adventurous. There is no need for packing a year's supply of dead pig, hundreds of sacks of flour, the odd mule, a gold pan and a shovel, then kissing the wife goodbye in the morning and going to work in the general direction of north for a couple of years, with the vague hope I'll be back at supper time in 1902.

As I walk along the ridge it curves into a mountain bowl and I disturb a couple of ravens which lumber awkwardly into the air on huge black wings until they catch the up-draught from the mountain and are transformed into aerodynamic masterpieces, effortlessly soaring and gliding. They were feeding on the remains of a caribou. As I approach the remains I see a lot of huge wolf tracks in the wind-blown snow and realize that a real live drama was going on up here when I was sheltering from the storm lower down. Caribou hair is everywhere, frozen into the blood-soaked snow. A blood-splattered antler lies off to the left, teeth having scraped white scars into its bronzed beam, and the tines at its top like a hand making a motionless grab for the sky in a plea for help. It is shocking and humbling to see all that remains of a majestic caribou which is designed to thrive and prosper in this brutal land as his ancestors have done for thousands of years. As I study the scene of death, the ravens alight on a nearby rocky outcrop to wait my passing while I wonder what final fatal mistake this poor creature made.

May 2004

Trying for Antimony Creek

Bridge and I are trying again today to master the cross country skis while Little Jack naps in the tent. The problem seems to be keeping the skis parallel. I can just about get going, but then one ski decides to turn left for Alberkerkie and I hurtle down the slope in an uncontrolled ark with skis widening and arms waving until the physical make-up of my knees can't take it any longer and buckle, felling me like an old dead tree in a storm. Bridge is mastering the art of turning; all she has to do is want to go in the direction she is turning. I'm getting a sore head mastering the art of stopping, but hopefully tomorrow I will be able to do it without the aid of a tree.

We are determined to get it right because the snow conditions have improved dramatically in the last week. A thick crust is hardening on the surface of the snow due to it melting slightly during the day and freezing hard at night. Tomorrow we intend to go into Antimony Creek. This is a large creek that falls sharply from the mountains to the east and drains into the North Klondike River. Judging by the map, there are a few old mining claims dotted along the creek and throughout the surrounding mountains, so it's obvious there is gold in them there hills and skiing could come in handy!

Little Jack is a constant delight in our lives, filling the days with joy, love and laughter, but Little Jack and a penny whistle are a constant nightmare, filling our days with headaches, ringing ears and shattered nerves. Take this morning: Jack awoke at first light, complained he was hungry then pretended his penny whistle was a machine gun and shot Boris with raspberries and flying saliva for half an hour. For Boris that was dramatic enough as he huddled by the stove, but for us it was painful because apparently you can't execute a sting operation on Boris with a tin penny whistle without considerable amounts of jumping on the bed and whoever happens to be in it.

Now it appears his tin penny whistle is actually a tin penny whistle, and his mum sighs with relief that he is not going to grow up to be Chuck Norris as he continuously blows it tunelessly in my ear while I do up his snow suit. Everything seems to take forever when Little Jack is involved but then everything is so much more enjoyable when he is.

Finally we are on our way skiing into Antimony Creek. I

have Little Jack in a pack on my back and Bridge is carrying the equipment. We ski down through the thick spruce forest lining the river valley and the snow is softer than we have found in the windswept mountains. Every time I turn around she's getting up. My heart goes out to her as she struggles out of the snow only to fall again yards further on but she is the one that keeps saying 'there's only one way to get experience'.

The deeper we go into the bottom of the valley the thicker the trees become and the softer the snow. Things become tougher the higher the sun rises. It's a warm day and we are sinking into three feet of wet heavy snow. Jack is still blowing his penny whistle in my ear as we force through the forest to the river. Boris is off somewhere barking at his demons; he's just light enough to run on the crust of the snow, with only the occasional foot punching through with all the flair of a Michael Flatly dance movement.

It must be the middle of the day, and we are exhausted when we dig a hole in the snow to light a fire for lunch. Jack has at long last remembered his penny whistle is a bazooka and shoots Boris with more enthusiastic raspberries and flying saliva when he returns to the smell of soup cooking. I catch Boris's eye as he sits by the fire and we give each other a knowing look that he or I are going to secretly loose the tin penny whistle.

After lunch we find a moose trail and follow it for a while as it winds its way through the thick trees. The going is slightly easier on the track but is still tough. At a break in the trees we come to the river which is still frozen solid. On the river the going is a lot easier. It's not only flat but the snow isn't as deep and is wind packed. We travel south for a while as the river takes us on its winding route through the forest. The sun is high, Little Jack has gone to sleep on my back and we are beginning to enjoy ourselves at last.

Once we leave the river and cut across country to Antimony Mountain looming in the sky at the mouth of the creek, conditions deteriorate. The snow is so soft that travel becomes almost impossible, so we reluctantly decide to return to camp and try again tomorrow. With a trail in this far, we should make better time in the morning.

Little Jack poured a cup of boiling water over his head this morning. He has burnt his forehead and the right side of his face, and his delicate young skin has just bubbled up and fallen off. It's really quite distressing. Bridge is curled up in the sleeping bag with him, softly singing Barry Manilow songs as he sleeps.

I've come looking for firewood as I hate Barry Manilow. The sheet metal stove in the wall tent is a necessary evil. We really need the heat it puts out but it takes up a lot of room in an eight foot by twelve foot tent because we have to keep everything away from it. Boris is the only thing that usually gets too close, and just last night he went howling out of the tent with his arse on fire. You'd think he would know better by now as he's got a permanent patch of short, different-coloured hair on his backside just above the tail, the result of years of sitting too close to the stove and singeing himself. Little Jack is usually really good around it. He knows it's hot and generally keeps away. Bridge only turned her back for an instant and he grabbed the mug of tea she had just poured from the kettle. He has a serious burn and poor Bridge feels terrible, but our problems are only just beginning as it's going to be a real challenge to keep the wound clean and moist because he has to wear a hat most of the time.

In the middle of the night the stove will suddenly take off and glow red hot, throwing embers out of the chimney like over-enthusiastic bridesmaids throwing confetti. Even with some old chicken wire shoved in the end of the pipe to catch the sparks we still wake up with burning holes in the roof of the tent, spreading in circles like mould on the surface of forgotten cream of chicken soup in the fridge. If we lost the tent it would definitely up the anti out here, but the heat is worth the risk.

We are camp bound for a few days until Little Jack heals. The weather is warm and the three feet of snow we are walking on is softening really fast so that life around the camp has become interesting. There is no way we can stand on the snow after mid-morning. Every footstep sinks three feet. Moving around is becoming tiring, for even the established trails to the outhouse and wood pile are soft and unpredictable. We have to wear snowshoes wherever we go and even they don't hold us up out of the snow. We sink probably two and a half feet instead of three and end up lifting the shoe out of the snow with fifteen pounds of wet snow on it. Winter is coming to an end and it's disappointing.

When Little Jack's face is healing nicely we try for Antimony Creek again, this time making an early start while the snow is firm. We reach the river in good time but we can tell the conditions are worsening every minute. Boris has even resorted to following our trail now because he too is sinking through the snow and wallowing like a coshed fish. The ice on the river is softer than before and overflow is a curse, icing up the underside of the skis. After an exhausting day we reach the point on the river that we think is opposite the mouth of Antimony. We can't see the creek because the river is braided in this section and islands of tortured willow stand in our way. With the conditions deteriorating there is no chance of us getting there today. We dig a hole in the snow and cook a meal. As the smoke from the fire rises and hides our view of Antimony Mountain, we know with a touch of remorse that this is the last time we are going to try to ski into Antimony this spring. Its secrets will have to wait.

May 2004

Hanging on to winter

I've decided for some bizarre reason to hang on to winter a little longer and ski up a valley that leads into the core mountain range of the area. The whole object of being here is to explore the country and look for possible geological features that might be worth investigating in the summer, but there seems to have been little exploring lately between burning faces, burning tails and burning muscles. My plan is to get high into the mountains by early morning while the snow is hard. Hopefully in the windy mountains the snow will be harder than in the valley where we're camped, and I can have a little snoop around for promising features and maybe camp the night or head down before the snow begins to soften.

I have no idea nor do I care what time it is but it's still dark when I leave, so it must be nearer the middle of the night than coffee time. There's not a cloud in the sky, but a bright moon, not quite full, is lighting my way with a silvery sheen and, like all the best magicians, has a backdrop of dark blue, studded with shining stars. There's something really different about skiing tonight. It's almost as if I shouldn't be. The mountains are so still, there is no call of the raven, chatter of ptarmigan or whisper of the wind, just a peace that seems heavenly, gentle, almost loving. The willows stand quietly like martyrs, bent over, holding their winter burden of snow that even the winter mountain winds have not managed to shake from their branches. I'm in a sparkling silver world with not a drop of colour anywhere. The air is chilled but not cold and I soon have to take off my hat and gloves. I feel as if I'm intruding as I head towards the blue shadows in the mountains, as if I'm catching them off guard and exposing as fraudulent their fearful reputation as soul takers, because at this moment they are far from fearful monsters, they are sleeping beauties.

After a couple of hours I dig a hole in the snow and stop for coffee. Daylight is on its way but the orange glow inside the Kelly Kettle is still the only colour as the small fire brings my brew to readiness. I honestly cannot think of anything I would rather be doing right now than drinking fresh coffee in the snow, looking down on a picturesque, moon-lit, wilderness valley. I cannot believe I have only recently discovered these abundant natural moments that I know should have been part of my life long ago. But I didn't know they existed because I was more interested in *Emmerdale* and *Coronation Street.*

It's so much easier going when the snow is hard and I glide over the top of it with very little effort and really enjoy myself. As the earth slowly rotates I watch daylight soak up the silver world around me. The moon has lost its potency to the sun which is still hidden below the mountains. The magical backdrop of deep blue star-studded sky has faded into a pale light blue.

It seems to be getting colder the higher I climb which is promising. As I reach the top of a small rise I disturb two bull caribou resting in the deep snow. They look worn out by the hard winter and an intense rut. Their majestic antlers have gone and their once silky coats cling to ribs and pelvic bones. They move reluctantly as if they're old men being asked to move seats by a teenage theatre attendant during the Sunday afternoon showing of *Bridge over the River Kwai.* I wonder if they will be able to keep ahead of the wolves and survive until the snow goes and the lichen, their main food source, is less of an effort to reach. They look as if they are hanging on for summer which is in total contrast to me who's hanging on to winter.

The mountains awaken gently, their jagged tops towering above me caressed by the sun. The valley is still dark and cold, the shadows deep and mysterious but begging to be explored. As the sun slowly peels them back like the dull, weather-beaten skin of an unknown tropical fruit, it reveals pink sparkling snow and my thoughts drift back to the tent where Bridge, Little Jack and Boris are curled up in a sleeping bag together. The stove will be low and a chill will have settled in the tent making the thin plastic outer layer of the sleeping bags stiff and brittle. The chill will be tickling faces and any carelessly exposed feet but it will need some serious reinforcements to get Bridge out of that warm bed to stoke the stove for morning. The thought brings a smile to my face because we try and take turns keeping the stove going all night, but unless the other one nudges you in the ribs and says 'It's your turn' when the chill starts to descend, it doesn't get done until the cold is unbearable; And it must be getting close to unbearable time.

At the top of the pass I stop. At this point I can see east and west for several dramatic miles. But the view north and south is blocked by vertical mountains that instill a sense of awe. The power of glacial ice is everywhere. These mountains used to be an igneous (solid bedrock) mound beneath hundreds of feet of sediment below a cold sea. The thought is mind boggling as I sit brewing Campbell's chicken noodle soup in a white sun-filled land. The sea eventually withdrew, and after billions of years its sediment turned to rock. Then one day a chilly snap blew in and stayed for centuries, and ice ages set to work freezing rock and forming glaciers that ground down the rock and dragged it away over thousands of years. The result is what I'm sitting on and looking at – scarred and broken rock, mountain faces ripped off, boulders the size of houses torn from their seats and cast adrift on the sea of ice and carried like galleons for untold years before being dumped where they happened to be when the tide slowed and melted away. At the end of short valleys curved walls of rocks or terminal moraines contain flat frozen lakes in gouged-out mountain bowls. Mountains with razor sharp ridges honed by billions of tons of grinding ice snake along the horizon as far as the eye can see.

As mid-morning approaches things really begin to warm up and the snow becomes too soft, so reluctantly I head back down the valley before the conditions really deteriorate. I try not to follow my own trail because I want to see the other side of the creek – you never know, there might lie the Mother Lode. I'm kidding myself, of course. I know that this gold hunting is just an excuse to answer the call of adventure, to sit in the shadow of mountains, to retrace the steps of mighty glaciers, to feel alive and fulfilled and to ultimately discover what we are made of. But it's a good excuse, and it's just like it was in the great stampede in 1898, when 40,000 people dragged themselves out of the depression of the 90s and headed north to the mystical land of the Yukon in search of riches. Most of them were ordinary everyday people who had desk jobs and lived in large cities, and wilderness to them was a city park with mallards floating on man-made lakes and daffodils bobbing beside cut grass. They had no idea what lay in front of them and most were ill prepared for the miles and miles of harrowing terrain. After a year of tortured journeying that took them over blinding glaciers, through tangled, wet forests and over sheer mountains, they must have known that they would not find untold wealth in deep, hidden Yukon valleys but would find it deep within the hidden valleys of their newly-discovered selves.

The lower I descend the softer the snow becomes, and it sticks to the bottom of my skis. I have to work harder going down hill than I did coming up. Ptarmigan, pure white save for their black tails, are everywhere and seem totally oblivious to a gangly Limey on skies trying to get out of the valley before things get difficult. The males in particular insist on puffing their chests out, spreading their tails and standing in my way like schoolyard bullies.

The sun is really bright and I can't believe how warm it is today. Every stride is an effort and I give up heading for the other side of the valley and concentrate on just getting out. I find a moose trail which is very handy and speeds things up a bit but I have no idea where it is going.

The snow drops in big plates as I ski over it. It's like a scene from a low-budget *End of the World* film where the hero is scrambling over rock that is cracking and falling away behind him. When I'm on the river the snow collapses about two feet and locks me into it. My skis, shins and poles are completely covered in heavy wet snow and I can't move an inch. I have never heard of this happening to anyone and have to laugh at the ridiculous situations I get myself into. I dig down to my bindings and manage to unclip my boots and stand out of my skis and immediately drop down two more feet. I am now up to my waist in wet snow and I am totally exhausted as I dig along the length of my skis and pull them from the grip of the snow.

I get trapped seven more times before I smell the wood

smoke of camp. It's early evening by the time I make it back. I have bad sunburn, I'm aching from head to foot and my shins and thighs feel as if the muscles are coming off the bone every time I move. It's time to let go of winter and put the skis away.

Snow, melted by the warm May sun, tumbles from mountains in jubilant creeks leaving behind blooming mountain flowers and greening tundra. The rivers are running, melting the jumble of thick winter ice. The eagles have returned and soar on thermals, fresh bear tracks decorate the stubborn snow along the river, the ptarmigan's heads are turning brown as they moult their winter mask and disappear in the emerging willows. It's time to head back to Dawson and see how the Yukon River looks. If it's this summery up here in the mountains, down in the valley it will be beginning to bloom. Reluctantly we pack up camp and say goodbye to the quiet, the ptarmigan, the great sky and the endless jagged mountains before heading for the low country of the Yukon River valley.

The Yukon River is free of ice and we can get to our cabin where the snow is all gone, apart from the odd heap lying like a sleeping cat in the shade. The place looks brown, battered and winter weary. The door creaks open and Boris immediately trots to the stove and sits down even though there has been no fire burning in it for a month. The window sills are littered with unfortunate flies in various stages of death which have survived the winter and come out of the woodwork, only to die in exhaustion and frustration against a window pane. A porcupine has dined out on a portion of the deck and two burying beetles are hurriedly burying a dead chickadee lying below the kitchen window. Bridge and Jack look tanned, fit and mountain weathered as they wander around the un-lived-in cabin. Jack is thrilled to discover his rugby ball isn't flat and enthusiastically runs outside, shrieking with delight, throwing the ball in odd directions and kicking the air in odder, unrelated ones.

We put a fire on in the stove and it quickly brings the cabin to life. It's nice to be home, but it feels threatened, and is a long way from the loneliness of the mountains. We have come back to the sound of chainsaws buzzing. A chap from town is building a cabin a couple of hundred yards away from ours and he wants to see the mountain, so he's felling trees like a retarded beaver. I try and explain about noise and privacy, but because he's never been here in winter he doesn't understand that in these forests during the winter a sneeze a mile away sounds like it's behind you. After all, it's summer, the ferry is in and things are easy. His main concern is that he wants to see the mountains from a window he hasn't yet built, so he's clearing the bush that can't be replaced in case it's in the way of his view. We watch and listen as our quiet world that has sheltered us from the worst of Yukon winters is mown down by the arrogance of man and a combustion engine – it's heart breaking.

SUMMER 2004

June 2004

The start of the search and the laying of plans

Little Jack is sleeping quietly in the June sunshine as Bridge and I talk late into the night beside our dying campfire. Boris is curled up next to Little Jack, and a whiskey jack is hopping around the camp picking up the last crumbs of Little Jack's biscuit that Boris has missed. We have come back to the North Klondike to search for gold on the gravel bars of the braided river and inflowing creeks. The weather is beautiful and the days almost endless. The river is still high from snow melt and is roaring its way through the forest, cutting banks, felling trees and dragging them with it on a hair-raising ride to the next log jam.

We have spent the evening discussing our options and have finally developed a famous Amos plan. This summer we are going to search the remote upper rivers and creeks for gold, working our way down to the Yukon River where we will look for a place to build a new cabin. 'When' we find good colours that have the promise of riches we will trace them back to the Mother Lode and become instantly rich, then build a boat, name it *Wise Mike* and sail to the wilds of Africa for a cold drink of Pimms out of a long glass filled with ice and listen to the roar of lions after the sun has dipped behind Kilimanjaro. I even promise myself one of those spiffy white hats and an arrogant British strut.

After a contented sleep filled with sunny sailing dreams we awake to another glorious day. I don't think we've seen rain for eight months. The red polls and crossbills are singing in the greening spruce. Dog roses creep through the forest floor, their purple buds not quite open, held aloft like an Egyptian caravan of priceless vases containing the royal wine. The roar of the river is muted by the tall dark spruce that are so much a part of these valley floors, standing for hundred of years and taking the full force of the Yukon's elements while sheltering the small and most vulnerable.

We are walking through a particularly thick patch of forest to get to the mouth of a creek to the north. Little Jack is on my back and shouting 'Moose pooh, Dadda' whenever he sees any, Bridge is behind carrying the supplies (again) and Boris is in front chasing a poor snowshoe hare that just happened to be in his path. The bush is thick and we put our heads down and push through it. I'm amazed at Jack who takes everything we throw at him in his stride. As I'm about to push past tight spruce boughs or through stubborn dog roses I say, 'Watch out, Little Jack', and he puts his little arms around his face and hugs the rucksack while I force our way through. Once out, I hear a muffled 'Okay Dadda?', and I assure him it's alright to look up so he can carry on his search for moose pooh.

We reach the mouth of the creek by mid-afternoon. The river seems more ferocious here as it takes a huge 90° bend to the west. On our side of the river a monster log jam shakes on the corner. Multiple trees, stripped of bark by the river and bleached white by the harsh sun, vibrate and creak with the force of the river slamming into them. Trees along the bank have toppled into the throttling current as the dark banks are cut away beneath. Some trees hang from the bank by a root with their tops bobbing in the current; every now and again one is sucked under and then released in a spectacular spray of water, and it's only a matter of time before it will join the torture of the log jam on the corner.

We make camp beneath a stand of poplar trees and brew up some Campbell's chicken noodle soup and feast on large chunks of bannock as we study the river and lay of the land around us. After our snack we take gold pan and spade and walk up the creek as it meanders through the trees into a quiet forested world. The water is crystal clear, and grayling dart for the darkness of the banks as we pass. Multicoloured rocks litter the bed of the stream and the occasional cluster of dead spruce needles spirals and waltzes on the surface of the water on its way through the quiet trees to the torment of the river.

I feel a tinge of guilt as I thrust the spade into the stream bed and a cloud of silt erupts into the water and drifts like a dark storm cloud down the creek. This creek has probably not been touched by human hand or foot. It flows peacefully from a gully in the mountains and drifts through the quiet forest to the river as it has done for thousands of years, channelling the melt from the mountains in an organized fashion and evidently not used to the bite of a steel shovel. I dig a hole in the rocks until I find fine material which I scoop into the gold pan and start the rather skilled process of panning while Bridge and Little Jack play I Spy on the bank. The water is incredibly cold on my hands as I slosh and spin the pan in the creek. This is the first time I've tried gold panning; it looks simple in *Paint Your Wagon* but there is a real knack to losing the larger debris and swirling the pan evenly so the gold stays in the bottom of the pan and is not washed out by turbulence. I struggle on, and although my Amos technique is effective in either washing everything or nothing back into the creek, I feel like I was born to pan. After washing out several pans and only getting a sore back and cold hands, my enthusiasm wanes a little so we wander further up the creek. We are looking for likely places gold could be trapped, a slow bend, a felled tree, a large rock or a long gravel bar, anywhere the current is slowed enough for the gold to drop out of the running water and become trapped in the gravel or in creases in the bedrock. As we follow the creek through the forest, stopping occasionally to pan out gravel from places that look promising, we are serenaded by the sound of fast running water. The water in this creek is slow and gentle but above all quiet, so we follow the sound through the trees until we find that this quiet creek is a backwater of the main creek that is jumping and jiving down the mountain in front of us, bringing with it, we hope, more gold from the weathered veins in the jagged summits. The backwater was probably once a major route for the creek until the main river changed or the permafrost melted elsewhere and diverted its course for ever. This vast land is constantly changing, moving and evolving like the wet paint on the canvas of a spirited artist, and we feel privileged to witness a moment in the history of the making of a masterpiece.

We brew up tea in the Kelly Kettle and lounge in the evening sun by the cool creek. Lying back on the forest floor, our dreams flow like the spring melt in front of us. It is exciting and exhilarating to be together as a family with nature in these forests. I watch Little Jack and Boris as they play on the bank. Boris is like a gentle Han Elder or 'Granddad' who quietly appreciates the value of the boisterous child pulling on his ears. Bridge hugs her warm mug of tea and loses herself, staring into the flowing water, her long black hair shielding her pretty brown eyes that reflect the sparkle of the creek. A woodpecker hammers into a spruce tree and its echo bounces through the forest as I watch my family and give genuine thanks that with this quest for gold there will come many more moments like this one.

June 2004

A change of plan after a close call

I'm nursing a dislocated thumb and bruised ego today. This morning I tried to cross the main river and rig up a rope to aid future crossings. At the narrowest spot we could find I waded out with the rope that dragged in the swift current and weighed heavily in my hands. I was facing up stream, had my backpack on and was grasping a hefty stick in front of me that formed a triangle with my legs. I was not even a third of the way across when the water was up around my waist and physically lifting me off the bottom. Anxiously I leant on my pole and moved a little further out as Bridge shouted undecipherable instructions from the bank. When the turbulent water was around my chest and numbing my legs I realised I might be in trouble. I stopped to think, as the current bounced me like a child's toy on and off the river bottom. I needed to undo the hip strap on my rucksack and let it go. It was far too heavy to cross the river with, and we could always find it down stream in a couple of days. However, I dared not release my grip on the pole which was steadying me while I was bounced off the river bed in the incredible current. The temperature of the river began to seep into my core as water pounded my chest, slapped my face and grabbed at my legs.

My next step was totally irrational and can only be put down to a dodgy moose sausage I ate for breakfast. I was tiring, and the cold was gripping my body and obviously affecting my brain because I leapt for the far bank like a water-logged Superman in the vain hope I might grab some tortured willows and drag myself ashore. Instead, I sank like the fat-head I am and tumbled along the river bed desperately trying to release my rucksack that now weighed more than I did and clung to my back like the 1970s wrestler Giant Haystacks in a heavyweight fight. At some point I hit air and gasped, saw willows and made a grab. I stopped myself for about point two of a second. The whole river took a shortcut through my nose and the force dragged me back under and into the current, dislocating my thumb in the process. I tumbled and bounced off boulders and hidden logs for a long way down the river, praying my rucksack wouldn't get caught on something. By pure luck, I managed to get another hold on the willows and, using pure adrenalin, pulled myself out of the frigid water and on to the bank where I sat for a while in total oblivion. I wasn't cold or feeling the bruises that patterned my body, but when Bridge finally came running up to me with Little Jack in her arms I realised whose faces were flashing through my mind while I was under water. Then the pain started, and the realisation that I was still on the same side of the river hit me like a ton of bricks.

Like all great plans ours seems not to be going to plan. The spring run-off is still high in the creeks, sending the river into turmoil and making it difficult to find the creek beds, never mind *Wise Mike* gold. So we have come back down to the Yukon River, borrowed an old wooden boat and are chugging up river in search of another home that won't be threatened by bigots, bullshit or bridges. We quickly loose sight of town and chug past the occasional outlying cabin. The cabins are small, hastily-built structures marking a goldmine, but they are all flying the Canadian flag from leaning makeshift flagpoles, the red of the maple leaf shinning brilliantly in the sea of greening forest. One of the many things I've noticed about Canadians is that they are obsessed with being Canadian. The radio says things like 'Every year smoking kills 40,000 Canadians', not 'people', 'Canadians'! They love to fly their flag and they do so with pride. It's great to see such patriotism, especially coming from England where the only time people dust off the flag is when the cavalry are away shooting tanned-looking chaps in a desert somewhere.

After our explorations of the small but hurrying mountain rivers during the past few months we have forgotten the sheer size and power of the Yukon River. At its narrowest point it is probably 100 yards wide. Swirling, hissing, silty water, the colour of milky coffee, hides varying depths of two to twenty feet, and treed islands choke the river course, making it difficult to find the main channel. We have to watch the water constantly for signs of hidden sandbars and 'dead men' (uprooted trees stuck in the sandbars) lurking just below the surface waiting to snap the propeller or ram a hole in the bow.

A dainty seagull joins us flying ten feet above our heads which delights Little Jack but distracts our attention from the river as we wait and watch for the inevitable, which happens, but splats on the deck missing everyone. It's bizarre to see a seagull way up here in the Yukon at this time of year, as we are hundreds and hundreds of miles from the sea and the salmon aren't running yet.

The wide openness of the river fills us with joy as we chug around islands forested with spruce, willow and birch. The sun is on our mountain-weathered faces and the warm wind is in our hair. I watch Bridge as she holds her face up to the sun with her eyes closed, her hair dancing around her tanned cheeks, her arms cradling Little Jack who dozes against the warmth of her body, and I feel blessed, I feel lucky and I feel alive. I remember how it was when we first felt the pull of this awesome river. This is the route we took when we first arrived in Dawson in 1999. We had, on impulse, decided to canoe from Whitehorse to the City of Gold 500 miles to the north. We had never been on a river in a canoe and we thought rapid was something that described heartbeats when we ran for the bus, but we had the time of our lives and arrived in Dawson with different souls.

Our route and experience mirrored that of the 100,000 gold seekers in 1898 who stampeded to the gold which shone brightly from the shadowy valleys of a mystical place called the Klondike. The hopefuls had no idea where the Klondike was. Many thought it was just north of Vancouver, some thought it was somewhere in Alaska, but all had absolutely no understanding of the thousands of miles of unmapped wilderness they would need to push through to reach it. They were ordinary people, bankers, salesmen, cab drivers, counter clerks and cobblers, but they all had something in common – a brave heart and a stubborn determination fueled by a strange fever charging through their veins that was brought on by gold. Thirty thousand men eventually reached Lake Lindemann at the headwaters of the Yukon River in the early spring of 1898, eight months after their departure. They had dragged their 'ton of goods' – enough food and equipment to last a year required by law for entry to the Yukon interior– northward for thousands of miles. While the ice slowly weakened on the quiet lake they built all sorts of crazy boats for the trip down the 500 miles of Yukon River to the Klondike and the gold. Some hauled their outfits to the lower Bennett Lake to get a head start on those building their boats on the shores of Lindemann. As they did so they passed through a boulder-strewn canyon which would claim many of the boats from the upper lake. A lonely wooden grave marker on top of the canyon is a stark reminder of this. It is of twenty-six-year-old John A Mathews, a farmhand from Idaho. John had tried twice to run the rapids the previous summer, but had lost everything he owned in the frothing canyon. After his second failed attempt he sat down on the bank in tears before wailing, 'My God! What will become of Jane and the babies?' and then blew out his brains.

On 29 May 1898 the rotting ice on the two lakes gave in to the warmth of the sun and broke free to float down river. Right behind it floated 800 boats with men straining at the oars and rigging up makeshift sails, all determined to get to the Klondike first. Forty-eight hours later 7,124 men were on their way down the river to the golden city. The boats filled the river for mile after mile in a strange, haphazard race, running canyons and rapids under the blazing Yukon sun.

Today, as we search for a new home, the river valley is slowly moulting its weary, shabby, brown colours as the green of spring paints a fresh masterpiece. Flocks of mallard, pintail and gadwall run along the water in front of us, their wings flapping until they become airborne and fly fast and low just above the water to disappear into back sloughs.

The ideal piece of land for our new home will be south facing, on a high bank of the river to avoid flood or ice damage, have large trees for cabin building and have a creek, full of grayling, to bring fresh mountain water to our door and provide an access route into the blue mountains snaking along the distant horizon. It sounds a tall order, but everywhere we look we find what we are searching for. We pull in to a likely spot and wander around, brew tea and think, 'This is exactly what we want', so we mark it on our map and continue to the next likely-looking spot and the same thing happens. By mid-afternoon we have a list of five perfect spots (one already has an abandoned cabin on it) and decide to turn back to Dawson to see if the pieces of land are vacant and available for staking.

July 2004

The strange hidden mountain

July has arrived and with it a heat wave that slows the pace of life almost to a standstill. With an average temperature of 26°C and the sun shinning almost twenty-four hours a day from an almost cloudless sky, it's no wonder the North Klondike River has dropped somewhat and we have been able to cross it with just a little excitement. We have discovered a small, narrow gulch that creases the north side of a jagged mountain that we haven't seen before. The mountain is smaller than its peers and lies tucked away on the snowy north face of the range, unseen unless you make the effort and cross the swirling river. We are camped by the river where the gulch flows in and we intend to climb the mountain by way of the gulch tomorrow. I have a strange feeling in my stomach and my heart pounds as I watch as a summer wind pushes thin wispy clouds which snag then tear open on the surrounding jagged summits... something is telling me this little mountain has a hidden secret men would kill for.

Another glorious day; this spring is the warmest we've had since coming to the Yukon six years ago. It is so nice after the long cold winter, but we welcome it with caution because although the mountain streams and North Klondike have dropped incredibly early this year making our progress easier, the forests are tinder dry and the chance of forest fires is extremely high. Although a natural cycle of the forest, fires are destructive and dangerous. They're usually caused by lightening (which is common during this hot weather) and can flare up in minutes and travel at incredible speeds through dry forest. Some fires are vast, covering hundreds of square miles and generating their own weather, making them totally unstoppable as they destroy everything in their path until the forest runs out. So as I say, we welcome the warmth with caution.

We don't get moving until mid-afternoon. Our camp is too

perfect to leave, with the morning sun sparkling on the clear creek, the smell of the new spruce buds in the air and the song of a multitude of unseen birds waltzing out of the cool forest. Little Jack spends most of the morning digging in the soft sand at the edge of the creek. I don't know how he can stand the freezing cold water but he splashes and dances in it for hours, his shrieks of delights and giggles filling our camp with life.

Eventually the lure of the strange mountain's secrets are too great and we begin to hike up the gulch. It is not very wide and is remarkably cool because the sun doesn't reach it until late evening. Thick clouds of mosquitoes erupt out of tangled willows which crawl out of the creek and make the going extremely slow.

Early evening we camp on an outcrop of rock away from the gulch. We are not even a quarter of the way to the snowy summit and we have been trudging for hours – these mountains always look small until you try to climb them. I dipped my pan in the creek a couple of times during the climb and found nothing but fools gold, but I have a real feeling in my heart that gold is here somewhere, lying in the confines of the gulch which snakes up the hidden north slope – sometimes you just have to have a little faith in what lies in your heart. Although men through the ages have come up with ingenious methods of finding gold from helicopters or boats, there is still no better way than trudging through the bush with the gold pan. This is what makes the Yukon and searching for gold so exciting for me. I would lay money no man has climbed this mountain or dipped his pan in this hidden gulch because it's far too hard to get to and it's only been a hundred years since the last rush which opened up only part of the country. There has just not been time to search this entire incredibly vast wilderness.

The hottest time of a Yukon summer day is around three in the afternoon and it must be about that time as we flop down next to the cool creek. We have been fighting our way up the narrow gulch through the thick willow but at last the brush seems to be thinning as we climb higher. I've dipped the gold pan in the creek all the way up and have found promising quartz and black sand, both of which are associated with gold; in fact, quartz is often referred to as 'the home of gold', but alas it seems the gold has gone down the pub.

Jack is thrilled to watch a whiskey jack glide on rounded wing out of the trees to land on Bridget's outstretched hand and gobble crumbs of bannock in her palm. Boris is lying on his side exhausted and panting like the Marlboro Man after running up stairs, while his tongue jives like an excited teenager newly awoken to the joys of the Bay City Rollers. I am nursing a twisted ankle, and now that the curtain of willows has parted, am struck dumb by the view. I have no idea how high we are but we are looking down on a vast valley running left to right before us.

Everything is a drama of time. Spruce trees spread out from the valley bottom and disperse into narrow gulches that curl up the sides of rocky mountains, twisted and gnarled by thousands of tons of ice. The mountains themselves seem to burst out of the trees as if they were a straightjacket too flimsy to restrain them. Glacier scars slashed along their sides are extreme and dramatic like the slash of a sword on the face of a victorious gladiator. I revel in the situation, soaking up the sun on my face, the mosquitoes humming around my sweated brow, my shoulders aching from carrying my son; the sweet smell of the willows, the endless sky, the laughter of Little Jack, the smile spread across Bridget's cheeks and the empty gold pan lying at my feet with black sand in its crease shout to me that we really are on the search for gold and getting close.

Sometimes I find life a little confusing. Until seven years ago I always thought I knew what I wanted, that I wanted to be successful, at what I really didn't care, as long as I could flash my watch, drive a *Saab 9000i* with no chips in the paint and buy a round in the bar without it hurting. Money alone would give me success. But finally in 1999 I discovered what I really want from life. I want a life studded with experiences and untold adventure. I want my son to know and love me for who I am, not what I do. I want my wife and my life intertwined and inseparable. I don't want to be wealthy with money, for no-one really cares. My ambition now, when I can no longer climb mountains, run rapids or mush dogs, is to sit on a deck in the sun and look back and remember the adventures, relive my life with honour and above all with deep, deep satisfaction. That is what I want... but the black sand drying in the crease of my gold pan stirs thoughts of riches, of wonder, of flashing my watch, of driving a Saab 900i, and it truly excites me.

July 2004

The wink of gold and the smoke of fire

At last! Ha ha! The glitter of gold is winking with unknown promise from the bottom of my gold pan. I can feel the excitement swell in my body as I stare at the glistening gold. It has been around for ten million years and gone on an unknown journey through this rugged land, unseen and untouched by human hand, and has now ended up in my pan as perfect as the day it was created. I shout to Bridge and Little Jack who are playing further up the creek. They see my excited and stylish jig and come running and peer in the pan together.

Bridge looks up and shrieks, 'It's minute!' Jack looks up and says, 'Moose pooh, Dadda?' I have to admit it is what is known in these parts as 'Fly Shit'. However, it is 'Golden Fly Shit'. Undaunted I state that it's the presence and the promise that is important, but they go back to playing anyway, and after sucking up the gold flake with my sniffer bottle and putting it in the poke I keep in my breast pocket, I go back to panning and dreaming.

Gold is gold, and now that I have it in my poke and burning in my heart, the spirit of the rugged Sourdoughs wells out of the water and takes me by the hand. The Sourdoughs were a breed of man not matched in modern society, and they didn't and wouldn't fit in. They endured indescribable hardship, starvation and disease, and made journeys regularly that we today think impossible. They were brave, hardy and independent men who travelled into the unknown and lived by their own rules. Many were successful and left the North wealthy. But many were driven mad or staved to death, unseen and forgotten by the unforgiving Yukon who took them into her swamps while their families back home hoped and prayed they were panning 10 cents to the pan from the creeks which run through the mysterious Great White North.

As I swirl my gold pan, my eyes watch the gravel washing out of it intently for any nuggets that my novice method is spilling back into the creek. It takes about ten minutes to pan out a good panful of creek bed to the fine black sand that holds the gold, but I find nothing, and try further up the stream where a bend creates an eddy behind a large chunk of rock. The eddy is deep and a lot of sand has built up in it so it looks promising. After panning out several pans of silt, my back is pleading to be straightened and the frigid water is cramping my hands when the sparkle of the gold is there again in the bottom of the pan at the end of a tapering swirl of black sand. It shines, wet and clear in the Yukon sun. I dip my index finger into the pan and the two virgin gold pieces stick to it and I bring them closer to my face for a better look. There really is something special about the sparkle of raw gold. Battered and rounded by water into irregular flat flakes, they are minute, probably worth 15 cents in total, but they are there on the end of my index finger in a glorious golden way, being touched by man for the first time in their billion-year history. But the best thing about them is the fact that they have come from somewhere, somewhere big, and they used this dark creek hidden in the bottom of the twisting gulch for their journey. Encouraged I dip the pan again. I look up into the shadow of the mountain. It is stern and quiet and I feel I have just learnt a secret it didn't want me to know as my eyes follow the gulch of the creek where it twists up into the lonely, snow-covered, north slope.

It is then that I notice the sky is smoky and my gaze is drawn east, down the valley. A huge column of smoke is rising from a bluff 15 to 20 miles away and drifting with the summer wind across the clear sky towards us. Adrenalin shoots through my body and I shout to Bridge and Little Jack who turn and look, Little Jack with amazement and Bridge with horror. A forest fire coming this way! We have to leave this mountain and get out of the valley. We are not in danger yet but we could be within a couple of hours. Forest fires wait for nothing. When they burn they rule with violent intensity and the world goes black.

We start back down the gulch at a hurried pace and before long the dreaded smell of wood smoke is floating in the air. The willows are thick so we can't see the sky or the column of smoke. All we know is we have to go through the smoke to get out of the valley and we pray the fire is a long way behind it. Willows are the most annoying of Yukon bush to push through. They grow at their own pace in their own direction which leads to an incredible mess. The first three feet from the ground up to their branches is caked in fine silt and other debris from the spring floods, so much so that as we push through them the fine dust is stirred up and sticks to our sweating faces and lines our gasping lungs.

When we are out of the gulch and on the main valley floor we see the sky through the quivering spruce. It is overcast with smoke and a warm wind casts burnt spruce needles into the trees like giggling maids throwing rose petals in their master's path.

Our truck is parked on the remote Dempster Highway and we need to get to it quickly, but the forest is thick and takes some pushing through. Boris, for once, is with us and seems to know he needs our help to get out as we walk into the hot wind that is unnerving the spruce above us. We cross the North Klondike, and this time Bridge looses her footing on a log and takes a dip in the shallows but otherwise we are alright. Bridge and I shoot nervous glances at each other as we try to remember the way back to the truck which also seems to be leading us towards the inferno.

A strange, dull night is cast by the immense column of smoke. Fighting panic we trudge through the forest, hopefully in the right direction. Little Jack begins to cry. He can sense our fear and is unnerved. He wants to be comforted but there is no time. He hangs to one side on my back and drips endless tears on the forest floor as we ignore him and push towards the road. To try to comfort him, Bridge starts to sings *Old MacDonald Had a Farm* which seems bizarre out here in the Yukon wilderness with the threat of a forest fire, but it could be worse, it could be Barry Manilow again, and I actually find myself shouting 'ee i ee i o' at the end of every verse as I climb over trees and push through the brush knowing they will be ash in a few hours.

Bridget's singing works as always and Little Jack is fast asleep in the backpack, oblivious now to our troubles, his tear-stained cheek resting on the nape of my neck and his right arm swinging with my gait. Eventually the forest opens and we find the gravel road and relief floods through our bodies. We jog the last mile to the truck under a brown sky raining burnt spruce needles. The air is acrid and close. The truck starts and we drive fast down the valley into the smoke column. I look back to see if I can see the un-named mountain whose gold is heavy in my breast pocket. Its lonely, snow-covered, north slope is hidden behind the veil of thick smoke and I can't help wondering if I really was getting too close.

We drive south at speed into the smoke. It's thick and dark, hiding the road, the valley and the fire. We see a couple of small fires burning on the side of the road but no main fire until we round a bend and see a wall of twelve-foot flames charging down the hillside to the east. Moments later the thick of the smoke is behind us and we emerge into a devastated world. It's as if someone pressed the 'red button'. Spruce trees once proud, united as a forest and standing strong, are now stripped naked and stand blackened and butchered, longing to fall, while the eerie glow of feasting embers lurks in charred root boles and under blackened bark. The ground smoulders like a First World War battlefield, the smell of burning life hanging in the air like a final eviction notice, and nothing, absolutely nothing is moving, not even the smoke.

July 2004

Staking our new home in burning hot summer days with no sun

July is staying very warm and more fires are burning throughout the Yukon, this area being particularly bad. Dawson is crouched under a cloud of smoke, the river blackened by burnt spruce needles from huge fires now burning all around. The buzz of helicopters is constantly in the air as the fires' progress is watched with nervous eyes.

Our cabin is getting smokier every day which adds to the difficulty of 34°C outside and 32°C inside, so there is no escape, no cool spot. The days are very long and for Bridge almost intolerable. She is lethargic and uncomfortable all day every day and longs for the cold of the winter. We haven't seen the sun for weeks because it's hidden by smoke which casts a strange glow over the land. We go down to the river most afternoons and cool off in the shallows and Little Jack loves it, panicking if he can't get his trousers off before he reaches the water's edge. Boris is also extremely lethargic and just stands in the cool water, occasionally taking a drink but mostly just standing.

The fires have people really worried. The town is on standby for evacuation, but where they are going to go, who knows, because we are completely surrounded by forest fires the size of Ireland and the only road out of town is closed because it is burning.

We have got word that the pieces of land we looked at on the Yukon River are open for staking and will cost $600 Canadian an acre. We are thrilled and can't wait to stake five acres of the perfect wilderness we found near a large creek 17 miles up river. I turn for help to a good friend, Jimmy Roberts. He is a native First Nation and this land is his traditional homeland. He is always ready for a challenge and has a sense of humour that makes every unreasonable request seem reasonable. He is tall, with peppered black hair and a mustache that hides a toothless grin. He is also a residential school survivor and carries a lot of pain with him, although he never shows it.

Residential schools were the work of the Anglican Church in the early 1900s. They tried to civilize and bring the fear of God to a Nation that, since the beginning of time, lived free with the migration of salmon and caribou. The Anglican Church, with the support of the government, collected native children (Jimmy, now fifty years old, was one of them, and is still in shock) and locked them away from their families for years, and they were beaten, raped, preached at and pontificated to, stripped of their culture, with their language and customs forbidden and literally beaten out of them, their personal privacy invaded at will by some (not all) perverted, sexually-deviant Christians in a role of trust. The stories are truly horrifying. When they were finally released as young adults, many of them required medical attention for their genitals. They knew nothing of their traditions or customs, could not speak their own language so could not talk to their families, and became alienated. Unable to communicate with their own families and shunned by the white man, they fled to the bottle because it was the only thing that listened while they burned with anger, humiliation and hatred.

Now, thank goodness, the Canadian government has relented slightly and the Han Nation, as they are known, are allowed to own land (a totally alien concept to them but they have to, to keep some of their homeland) and they have their own recognized government, but as a nation with rights and culture they will unfortunately fight forever the flood of the fickle, plastic world of the white man who thinks he knows best.

Jimmy is delighted to help as always. He is probably the only man in the world who makes me belly laugh uncontrollably for hours with his comments, and those comments fly as Bridget, Little Jack and I climb into his boat and head up river into the smoke to stake our new home.

The smoke is thick in the warm summer air as Jimmy throws open the throttle and the boat rears up to glide over the water at speed, the warm wind spreading his cheeks into a mischievous smile that they really don't need. About ten minutes up river the smoke is so thick we can't see the banks and Jimmy slows the boat to a chug. Apart from the seven years locked away in residential school, he has lived on the river all his life so knows it like the back of his hand. His people are river people who lived well on the salmon that swim its length, and his movements and thoughts echo his elders as he negotiates the sand bars, back sloughs and islands.

As the smoke becomes even thicker, almost choking, it is evident that we are heading towards a fire, and I watch him with interest as he searches blindly through the smoke for the main channel. I fight anxiety and look at Bridge whose face is showing signs of concern as she sings to Little Jack in her arms, but Jimmy never once questions our logic, our reason or our sanity as a white man would at this point. He simply genuinely wants to help us because he can.

After chugging blindly up river for about an hour, I see through the smoke the two small islands that protect the piece of land we are looking for from the main river. As several ducks take to the air on frantic wings we turn into the slough, Jimmy cuts the engine and we glide quietly to the bank.

Nothing is moving and the quiet forest shouts to us. We can't see the tops of the spruce as smoke swirls through them on wind of its own making. This place is the pick of the locations we selected for our home and it's the most beautiful place in this whole rugged land. It's softened by dog rose and poplar trees and sheltered by huge spruce. It's sung to by a small creek which ripples out of jagged white mountains far off on the horizon and it's continually stroked and soothed by the Yukon River flowing by its south-west bank. Jimmy helps me stake roughly five acres that will give us views, fresh water and logs for a cabin, while Bridge and Little Jack cool off in the slough, their laughter tumbling through the quiet forest. During lunch I ask Jimmy why he doesn't have an outhouse at his cabin. He looks at me squarely with dark eyes, then squints into the surrounding forest and says, 'I'm like a dog, I crap in my neighbour's yard', and his black moustache straightens and his gravelly laugh echoes through the smoky spruce. I laugh too, but I take a moment to admire him because, after everything he's been through, he still is who he was meant to be.

I am in the mountains on my own, prospecting, while Little Jack, Bridge and Boris stay home at the cabin and cool off in the river. Just before I left, I went to town for supplies and became a little unnerved. I have no idea how much, if any, danger we are in, but everybody is talking about evacuation and losing everything in a fire storm. Apparently around us four and a half million acres are burning which is nearly four per cent of the Yukon's land mass. Firefighters are being flown in from all over the country and they hang around town in bright yellow jumpsuits covered in soot and carry crackling radios on their belts that suddenly burst into life with things like 'Aaah, Tango one nine are you out there? We need some TLC on this FBF with a B49.' The air is thick with smoke and water bombers roar constantly as they take off every five minutes from the tiny airstrip. We haven't seen the sun for weeks which is heartbreaking, because the summers are so short and the sun is with us for such a brief time.

This mountain area I have come to is new to me. I can't go back to the hidden mountain with the secret gulch because a huge fire is billowing smoke at its base and roaring along its east slope, so I am walking a razor-sharp mountain ridge further north and it's leading me into a Never Never Land of jagged rocky mountains, hidden alpine lakes and tumbling streams. The view would be amazing but I can only see a couple of hundred yards in the smoke. The ridge is so sharp I have to walk placing one foot in front of the other, holding my arms out to steady myself and hoping my heavy pack doesn't overbalance me and send me hurtling down the mountain to the tundra far below.

I find a fossil of some sort of clams all clustered together. They look just like a bunch of shells in mud so it's striking to realise they are all rock. A group of seven caribou bulls walk fluidly along the lower slope as I cut down towards a lake. Their antlers are huge and look even bigger because they are still in velvet.

The smoke in the valley is not as thick but does steal the mountains' splendour by cutting off their heads. This small alpine lake is remote and deserted apart from the odd marmot whistling. The quiet is profound and the stillness soothing. It is so beautiful. A multitude of waterfalls tumble into the lake from a glacier hidden in the base of the mountains at its western edge, but I can see evidence of harsh times: a caribou skull, grey and stone-like, juts out of the tundra; stunted willows growing on the leeward side of large rocks crouch like war-torn soldiers waiting for the order to charge; and pitted snowdrifts, shouting winter warnings through the silence, still lie in dark folds of the granite mountains.

I dip my gold pan into the creek where it tumbles out of the glassy lake. The mountains, moody with contorted shadows on their flanks, stand in a semi-circle behind me and the valley flows out to the west. I can't see the whole valley which cuts a wild path through the mountains because it drops sharply after the lake plateau but I can see its ancient path leading into the smoky haze.

I half-heartedly pan out some silt. I don't want to find anything. This is a beautiful, peaceful place and really should not be dulled by the shine of gold. I can't bear to watch the silt from the pan clouding the pure mountain stream, never mind the thought of digging a hole in the place. I return to my small camp by the lake and watch the mountains as I drift in and out of contented sleep... this is heaven.

As July draws to a close the fires are still raging and getting much worse, the smoke is dense and acrid and people are panicking. The Gold Fields are burning and the miners have been evacuated to town, the Han Nation has evacuated some of their elders who have difficulty breathing to Whitehorse, and everybody is wondering what is happening 'out there'. The road to the south has reopened but is still under threat from another fire and may close at any moment. An Emergency Measures Meeting is being held in the town hall to discuss a way of getting everybody out. We decide to leave while the road is open. Hurriedly we pack the truck with most of what we own and bury the rest in a clearing. We say a reluctant goodbye to the cabin and drive through the smoke to the 'outside', unsure whether we will have a home on our return.

AUTUMN 2004

September 2004

Returning home and back to the search

Butterflies in our stomachs make us squirm as we drive through miles of burnt and devastated spruce forest into Dawson at the beginning of September, unsure what we will find on our arrival home. Smoke is still in the air but not as thick as it was a month ago. The tops of the spruce are already slightly purple from the bite of frost, birch leaves are turning yellow and the sky is lined with the Vs of sandhill cranes heading south. When we cross the river we see no blackened spruce needles in the water and the trees on the far bank are green and untouched. Our cabin has survived and stands golden in the evening sun as we arrive. It feels wonderful to be back and we all slip instantly into the groove of Yukon life after the bustle of the outside world.

At the first opportunity we head off and cross the North Klondike to hike to the secret mountain and its hidden gulch. The march of autumn is in full swing at this elevation. Birch trees are golden and splash red and yellow into the spruce-green valleys. Clinging to the lower slopes of the mountains, just above the tree line, tundra glows a rusty red, while a thin layer of brittle ice grows from the banks of mountain creeks and midstream boulders. Aloft the skies are turbulent and the mountaintops brood silently with the stern face of winter. The smell of forest fire smoke is still in the air and many miles of spruce lie naked and burnt. In some areas the soil is completely burnt down to the sand and gravel under a thick layer of ash, in others islands of spruce stand tall and green with only their outer needles singed by the intense heat of the main fire as it somehow missed them.

As we climb the gulch a real mountain cold stabs our bodies and we realise time is running out because we are now climbing directly into winter. We brace against the wind and climb higher, the glitter of gold from this gulch driving us up to unknown heights, fuelling our passion and encouraging us to fulfill our dreams, safe in the knowledge that fighting the cold and this mountain is all part of living them. This is what it's all about, the cold, the wind, the race against winter and the glitter of raw gold. Our spirits soar with the eagles because we have a real purpose in climbing this mountain. It's no longer purely for adventure or 'because it is there', it's for the real chance that a fortune in gold may lie in the folds of rock that make up the north face. Fire and flood have kept us away from this place, but we are back undaunted, fighting the mountain winter, forcing upwards and breaking the ice on the creek eddies, tracking the tantalizing gold that we feel sure has been stripped from a secret place high on the summit... And it feels wonderful!

The sun drops quickly behind the horizon and the cold air bites our faces. Moments later Little Jack, who never complains, starts complaining about the cold. It is then Bridge pours cold water on the fever that burns within me and heads back down to the weather-butchered tree line while I try one last pan. As I dip the pan my hands are numb from the freezing water and my face is sluggish in the cold mountain wind that blasts from the north, but I swirl the pan and float the dross into the creek. I feel gold below my feet, I know I do and I know I'm close. I gradually swirl the gravel out of the pan until the black sand lying in a thin curve arches across the bottom of the pan. Not a hint of gold winks from the dullness, and anger suddenly surges like a demon through my body. I'm shocked, and fight aggressively to squash it. That was the last pan this year. We need to get back to the warmth before night locks us in up here.

I look down into the tree line and see a wisp of smoke in the haze of night. Bridge has a fire going and Little Jack will be warm as they sing and rock together in the firelight. As the stars begin to show, I turn, fighting guilt, and climb with snow under my feet to the next eddy. I break the ice on the creek and fill the pan once more. Darkness is blotting out the valley and snow flits on the wind as I try to concentrate on the pan.

I need the glitter of gold, any gold; I need it like a kiss from Little Jack. I need it to lighten my path back to the tree line, I just need it. But above all as I sit here alone, in the dark, on this barren, windswept mountain, I need it to stop the Yukon feasting on the flow of hope draining from my soul.

I can't feel my hands at all when the last pan from the last possible place has washed down the creek leaving behind nothing but cold misery. I fight disappointment and the tide of failure harder than I fight the cold wind buffeting my body. I stand with a sigh and put the gold pan and shovel on my pack and begin the descent in the dark to the comforting glow of Bridget's fire. I was convinced this mountain had a heart of gold but the Yukon wins again; after all, it's her show, it's her beauty and it's her gold, but why does she always pretend I have a chance? I stop on a precipice and look into the sky. The stars are out but snow clouds are billowing over the next ridge threatening their sparkle. I'm tired and demoralized as I yet again reluctantly release my ego to the Yukon and yet again she snaps it away on an icy wind.

When I arrive at camp Jack greets me in the orange glow of the fire with the sort of hug only a three-year-old child can give. He doesn't kiss me because he hates my beard but Bridge does and both warm me immediately. I linger on the fringe of camp enjoying the effect of the warmth of the fire and the warmth of my family while the wilderness creeps up my back and pokes me with menace, goading me to try again... if I dare.

September 2004

Down from the mountain and back at our cabin in need of wood

The Yukon River valley is a different world from the mountains. There is no snow, autumn is in its glory, the birch trees are golden and their leaves are floating like petals in a parade on the stiff breeze. The sky is full of sandhill cranes flying south, and bald eagles hang around by the water's edge picking at salmon carcasses. The tops of the spruce trees are purple from the bite of frost giving the only colour to the brownness. It's not until the sun dips behind the mountains that we know something huge is about to happen. That is when the temperature drops considerably in the birch-golden valley, when ice creeps out of the ground and skates over standing water imprisoning it for months, when the cold hardens the ground, stiffens trees and kills the flow of creeks in deep gulches, and that is when the mountains come to us.

I walk out onto the deck with a cup of tea early in the morning. It's so quiet. The light of the day has seeped into the darkness, shadows are creeping back into the trees, a whiskey jack flies onto the railings for the last of my breakfast bannock and a raven watches me from his perch in an aspen tree. I notice a sharpness to the air, my face tingles, my hands feel cold and Boris's breath is steaming as he lumbers onto the deck after a futile chase with squirrels. I also notice the scouts of winter frosting the trees and strangling the grass... something big is coming and it's made it over the mountains from the north.

The coming of winter seems early and we are not ready for it, but then we wouldn't be because we spent last month in England where we were engulfed by greenness, roundness and kindness. On our route to escape the fires we flew back to England. We saw round, leafy trees and green hills, patchwork fields and ornately caved buildings with pillars, we saw men in suits and ladies with handbags and everyone was talking with cell phones. We saw the smiling faces of family and friends. We met two-year-old nieces and played firemen with three-year-old nephews. We drank fine whisky out of cut-crystal glasses with proud Grandpas and coaxed war stories out of Great Aunts drinking grape juice in sunny gardens. We saw nothing, absolutely nothing that was sharp, jagged, harsh or cold. It was a wonderful trip and it was great to be surrounded by family again, but it cost us. Not only did it use up the last of our savings but it has left us totally unprepared for winter, and now my heart sinks as I look at the woodshed and see no wood. I look at the meat-shed and see no meat, and I look around me and see nothing round, nothing shiny and nothing smiley. All I see is jagged spruce, jagged mountains and jagged weather with cold tumbling over the mountains as I speak.

These cold mornings and longer nights dampen the fever of gold. Our thoughts are of the struggle ahead, of our work for heat and meat. One shed full of wood and a moose hanging in another are like money in the bank, and both will last us well into next May when the water is running again, the garden is started and the sun is endless. Right now next May seems an awful long way off and a dead moose and a good fire are far more important than the cold glitter of gold. Reluctantly we cast the fever into the chilled air and load the truck with camping gear, chainsaws, gun and Jack's toys and go in search of wood and moose.

In an old burn left by a forest fire years ago we find what we are looking for – a good supply of standing dead spruce trees. They are dry and clean and hold a lot more BTUs than the poplar we have been burning lately. The comfort of the winter is related to the firewood we have in the shed. If we burn poplar we feel the cold creep into the cabin during the nights because the fire has gone out in the stove. If we have spruce or birch the cold is kept from the cabin until the early morn because the fire burns longer and hotter, so we are pleased to have found this stand of spruce and we relax slightly.

I play *What's the time, Mister Wolf?* with Jack as Bridget tackles the job of felling the spruce and cutting them into eight-foot lengths. Jack loves *What's the time, Mister Wolf?* and giggles with delight as I step closer and closer. He really is lucky to be three – he's totally oblivious of the fact that the main reason we're playing is to keep him out of the way of his mother with a chainsaw. His eyes sparkle as he chases me, instead of me chasing him, it's so much fun – he never was one for rules (just like his mother).

When Bridge gets hungry we boil up some Campbell's chicken noodle soup and dip bannock into it. It tastes great as we sit in the forest and listen to the cranes cackling as they fly south above us. The air is cold but not brittle, but I do notice Jack's cheeks are getting red with cold so I put a face mask around them which he immediately fills with chicken noodles and bannock – oh well.

After lunch Bridge goes back to felling trees and Jack and I read *Fat Charlie's Circus*. Bridge and I have learnt over the years that our partnership takes working at. It is vital that both of us can do all the chores. In a partnership that is so unbalanced in physical strength such as ours – I am six feet tall and 14 stone, Bridge is five feet tall (maybe) and weighs less than a portion of Super Size Chicken McNuggets – it's so easy for me to do all the strenuous chores and Bridget all the easier ones. This we found leads to all sorts of problems, frustrations and conflict. Bridge was always stuck inside doing the washing up while I was always outside in -40°C trying to start the snow-machine – both of us frustrated, and leading to Bridget not learning to do some of the chores. If either of us goes away, we need to know the other can handle all things, from making porridge to de-icing the floats on the skidoo carburetors at -50°C.

Although Bridge is nervous about felling large trees, she takes on the challenge with immense dignity. She knows she has to be able to shoot, gut, chop, start, cut, split, pull, drag or fix anything up here, otherwise she would be reliant on someone else and that's not always possible. I watch her walk through the trees with that huge orange chainsaw swinging in her tiny feminine hands and I wonder what she would look like in a ball gown because she looks perfect against the golden birch.

It takes a couple of days to cut the trees and haul them back to the woodshed. The feeling of relief that we have wood is uplifting and revitalizing so it doesn't take us long to get started on the task of bucking and stacking the huge pile of logs we have accumulated in our yard. We need about ten cords of wood (a cord is a stacked pile of logs eight feet long, four feet wide and four feet high) to get us through an average winter, and it's really wonderful, but not always possible, if we can get all ten cords cut up and stacked in the shed before the snow flies.

September 2004

Moose hunting with Gord

On this day, 24 September, twelve years ago, for some reason that escapes me now but was probably the result of far too much cough medicine, I took Bridget on a romantic weekend to Burton-on-Sea. We walked the deserted beach arm in arm laughing at the endless rain and eating long-dead cockles soaked in vinegar from a Styrofoam cup. And it was there, for a joke, that we saw a clairvoyant by the name of Madam Dora, and if I remember correctly she was in desperate need of a new couch. Bridge and I sat down on it and sank to the floor and there we stayed for half an hour, imprisoned by fire retardant foam while the so-called Legendary Madam Dora wafted dramatically about the room, distinctly lacking in crystal balls, and told us that Bridge would be a beautiful, natural person who followed her instinct and desires and I would be a second-hand fridge salesman in Wolverhampton with a burning ambition to sing in the *Songs of Praise Christmas Special* from Glastonbury Cathedral.

As it turns out, the Legendary Madam Dora was right about Bridget who, since being seven years in the Yukon and subjected to its brutal realism, beauty and hardship, has blossomed from a caterpillar trying to survive a money-driven, image-conscious world into an amazing butterfly that attracts light, laughter and sincere love wherever she wanders. I, as a result of the thirty-minute interlude on a knackered couch with Madam Dora, have developed a nervous twitch whenever I'm near anything that makes ice cubes and still have severe trouble in controlling my impulse to shoot Aled Jones with an anti-tank missile as soon as he starts singing about walking anywhere, never mind in the air with God-Damned Snowmen!

Nowhere in Madam Dora's pontifications was the mention that twelve years to the day I would be sitting on a rapidly freezing moose head, in an inflatable raft, floating down the

Stewart River in the middle of the Yukon wilderness, having not seen an electrical chilling device in years and having not one single desire to sing a chorus line from *Glory Halleluiah*. However, if she had said that I would be, I have to say I would have told her in no uncertain terms to get a crystal ball, lose the leopard leotard and then demand my fiver back.

Burton-on-Sea, the rain, the smell of chips, the call of the sea gulls and the stench of the harbour all seem such a long way away as my buddy Gord and I drift down an isolated river in the middle of the Yukon Territory with our dead moose. Gord and I ventured this far into the Stewart River country because we both needed a moose and there was a rumour that the Stewart River had lots of frisky moose on it at this time of year all flaunting and fighting for the females.

So with all the usual planning I put into these things I jumped on a raft with Gord two days ago and went in search of a frisky male moose with the intention of cutting its head off and sticking it above the fireplace, then making sausages, steaks and stew out of the rest if it. At this time of year when the sky is dark at night and the snow floats ominously in the air, meat is a real concern. One moose can feed Bridget, Jack and myself throughout the winter and, if we can keep it frozen, well into May. So Gord and I came on a shopping trip and found what we were looking for yesterday, in the wilderness isle next to the pine fresh. After about nine hours of rowing we saw 700lbs of fireplace ornament, rump steak, prime rib, stew, and sizzling sausage on a gravel bar taking an evening drink from the river.

We pulled the raft onto the bank about half a mile from the moose and managed to sneak to within 100 yards of it. Just as we were about to shoot, the moose turned into Linford Christie and took to the hills. I was in a state of shock at how 700lbs of sausage can actually run on long spindly legs moving every direction but east when Gord dropped to one knee and fired. The moose gave up the chance of gold and sat on its haunches, then toppled over with a thud. We waited. It didn't die. Gord shot again and placed a bullet into its neck piercing the moose's jugular and sending its giant head flicking back over its shoulder only to flop back with a clatter of antler onto the river rock where it lay. We waited again. Then, adrenalin pumping, we cautiously approached the dying animal. It watched us with terrified cow eyes as its life drained onto the river bank with its blood. We were about to shoot again when the blood from its neck slowed to a drip, its tortured eyes rolled back showing the white, its legs went limp and the gentle cow eyes reappeared with the dullness of death. We, Gord and I, had killed it. We had killed a strong natural animal that had not known us, seen us, liked us or loathed us. It had not bothered us, interrupted us, disrespected us, challenged us or crossed us... but we killed it because we needed the body that worked it. And I linger on that point daily because I don't want it to be like buying a pound of pork chops, I want it to be hard, raw, real and respectful... which it is. The killing of a moose is such a dramatic moment. It represents a lot of things. Not only does it relieve the pressure of getting meat for winter but it reveals with sudden stark violence the real cost of living with nature. Hunting down and killing your meat is the ultimate act of a natural way of life in the North. An old-timer once said to me, 'The first time I shot a moose I cried, I was a broken man. The first time I ate that moose I cried, I was a happy man.' And that is what it is like living with the Yukon and not against her. She is cold, brutal and callous one minute, then warm, beautiful and generous the next... but she always makes you cry.

It was dark by the time we butchered the moose and packed it onto the raft and in that time we had got to know it. We both said thanks genuinely, unashamedly and honestly many times. It's a harsh moment that I try and remember whenever a piece of the moose is eaten because it keeps the thing real.

However, we are now bear bait. We are covered in blood and stink like 700lbs of steak and sausage. A dead moose to a bear is like Guinness to an Irish pub singer. As we float down the beautiful quiet river we can see bears feeding in the surrounding hills, and when we drift past they lift their heads and smell the air in excitement and some of them are over a mile away.

Last night was a nightmare; we were exhausted by the time we got back on the water so we only rowed across the river from the kill site and made camp. We had not even had time to light the fire before a fox came waltzing into camp like a short policeman issuing a seatbelt ticket and made a bee-line for the raft to tug at the moose. We shouted and threw some stones but it was apparently as deaf as Boris on a lead. It was only by running at it and shouting flamboyant obscenities that the fox decided it wasn't the thing to do and quickly ran into the night. I hadn't turned my back a minute when it was back, tugging at the moose like a terrier. Again I launched at it, throwing stones. It didn't leave for the trees until I was almost upon it. I couldn't believe it. I was on my way back to the fire when Gord came running past me throwing stones because the fox was back again. We didn't want to shoot it but really began to think we might have to. Instead we gathered up arm-loads of stones and as soon as the fox reappeared, which wasn't long, we began throwing them at it. It sat down and watched just out of range. It literally walked between us and the tents in a straight line as if we weren't there. It was bizarre. In the end we gave up and let him dine on the premise that he was only small and could not physically eat that much, but I can honestly say that cheeky fox ate more meat than a skinny Mara hyena first upon a dead hippo.

As we sat by the fire we could hear the wolves fighting over the gut pile and other scraps at the kill site across the river. The night had a chill to it and was very dark which added to our nervousness. We talked about staying up in shifts to protect the meat but in the end we were both too tired for any such macho behaviour and crept into our tents with loaded guns. It must have been a few hours later when I was awoken by the sound of something very large and strong crossing the quiet river towards our camp. I held my breath to aid my hearing and my ears strained for any clue as to what was now shaking itself by the raft. Then I heard a low whisper. 'Dorian, are you awake, did you hear that?' Gord was obviously as scared as I was. Whatever it was began to walk up the shore towards our tents, the round rocks that littered the shore grinding and rolling as whatever it was stood on them. I grasped the rifle and my fingers searched for the safety. It was then that the call of a lonely and amorous bull moose shook the tent, followed by the rhythmic grunting that is suppose to show how sexy he is. The bull moose wandered right between our tents and up over the bank behind us, grunting with every step and calling into the night. We relaxed slightly and once again tried to get some sleep. Then near daybreak something that I can only presume was a black bear sniffed my tent loudly, gave a snort of surprise then a woof of disgust and charged back into the woods. Consequently we were on the river before dawn this morning with no coffee or cornflakes, our goal to row to Dawson, a distance of 150 miles, within two days.

Camping on the river with a dead moose and Gord is not one of my better moves. I thought I was really getting the hang of this adventuring business – after all, it doesn't take much cognitive thought. In fact, the less I think cognitively the more adventure I seem to have, but to find myself as bear bait in unknown territory after seven years in the Yukon shows I should have stayed a dyslexic cartoonist in Polppero.

We are going to have to camp again tonight. It's already getting dark and we are exhausted. We are taking two-hour shifts on the oars, but after ten hours it's tiring. I'd rather be rowing, because sitting on a freezing moose head on a raft in late September on the Stewart River, which is what Gord and I have to do when not rowing, is not the warmest of pastimes and being cold for two hours is enough to wear you out more quickly than dancing to a Yazoo song.

Just as dusk has stolen the distant spruce and steam swirls from the river Gord steers in to the bank. We make camp quickly, each knowing our roles. Gord cooks the first warm meal of the seventeen-hour day while I pitch the tents and start the fire. As we sit by the fire sipping bad whisky out of chipped tin mugs with our stomachs full of moose and our backs cold from the chilly autumn night, Gord says, 'Ya got blisters?' I have to admit the palms below the fingers on both of my hands are weeping blisters. He takes off his glove and shows me his right palm in the firelight. It's like the US Embassy wall in Baghdad. Now we both have blisters our pace will be slowed. We have no real idea where we are except somewhere on the Stewart River. We're not lost because the Stewart drains into the Yukon and that will take us right to Dawson if we are awake; if not, we'll float past and the next stop is Eagle, Alaska. We will obviously have to camp another night or so, and it's a little unnerving because each night we camp is like being shrimp on the barby for bears and the sheer distance we have to cover to reach Dawson is demoralizing.

The following morning we heave a huge sigh of relief because the night was pretty uneventful and we get on the river again after a breakfast of moose liver and strong black coffee. It didn't snow in the night but this morning is one of those days that shout: 'You'd better put what you need before May under cover!' The cloud is low, the river is steaming and there's frozen snow floating in the air. Daylight has just arrived but it's difficult to tell because the steam mixes with the cloud to form an opaque grey canopy just above the spruce tips. Everything is silent and beautiful. The dead moose, Gord and I say little to each other as we drift through amazing country on the silent river.

The water is gentle compared to many rivers in the Yukon but we pass evidence of dramatic spring floods and the immense pressure of flowing walls of ice. Dozens of trees lie twisted and broken high up on the banks at some of the bends, so intertwined they have become one in a spectacular natural sculpture. The aftermath of the power of unstoppable water is everywhere, from gravel bars honed like the blade of a much-loved hunting knife to banks undercut so deeply that the top layer of scrub and trees, held together by root mass alone, curls and breaks into the river like a child's sand castle at high tide. The evolution of the river is evident at every stage and turn. The river ripples through the land like a slow-motion circus whip, cutting its way through the forest. We see ancient, once frozen, log jams that have filled with silt and long since turned into riverbanks upon which a forest of trees has taken root and thrived for hundreds of years until the river for some reason has changed its mind and has turned back and begun to cut into them again, exposing the tangled mass like bones from a robbed grave. We see single uprooted trees that have floated with the ice like galleons, riding the rapids and navigating the swollen river until the water drops and their twisted roots begin to drag like a slipped anchor through the gravel bars until their eventual wreck. Held firm by the root bole in the gravel, the tree wafts for a while with the current, until silt collecting in the branches on the downriver side cement the tree to the earth once more and start a new island.

The wildlife is abundant. We see bears feeding on the hillsides, eagles catching jumping fish, wolves trotting along the bank and beaver squabbling within log jams. But there is a presence on this river which is making the hair stand up on the back of my neck. Occasionally we see old, long-abandoned cabins. Some have caved-in mine shafts by the door. They are the remains of the dreams and hopes of rugged men who came north in search of gold. On one bend we see a shaft exposed by the river, its log sides neatly intertwined to support the walls now standing like a tower out of the bank. It shouts courage, adventure and following dreams.

No one really made a huge fortune on the Stewart River (although some have and still do on inflowing creeks). It is known as a grubstake river. That means a prospector can find enough gold from the gravel bars to secure his grubstake for next year, the term grubstake being given to the year's supplies that are lent on condition of payment later. I long to stop on one of the many gravel bars and sink a shovel to the pay dirt, but time is of the essence and every daylight hour is needed for negotiating the river.

It's late afternoon when we enter the much faster Yukon River and our pace increases slightly which is nice because both Gord and I are fading and our blisters are incredibly painful. When we can no longer see the river in the gloom of the coming night, we find a campsite. It's not perfect but it will do. As I'm putting up the tents I see a fresh bear track in the sand along the shoreline and hope it's not an omen of what's to come. The night is quiet and dark and we eat our moose and stare into the crackling fire for about an hour, lost in our own thoughts. But with full bellies and aching muscles, tiredness sweeps over us and we drag our bodies into our tents.

Hours later I am awoken with a jolt by what sounds like chunks of meat being dragged off the raft and hitting the water with a splash. Both Gord and I leap out of our tent with loaded guns. We can just make out the outline of the raft but nothing else in the dark night. Anxiously we wait for a sign of what is happening. Then a similar splash hits the water ten feet from where Gord is standing. It's a beaver splashing its tail on the water in warning and not a huge grizzly bear gorging itself on our meat. Relieved we return to our sleeping bags for the rest of a fretful night.

We are on the river early and an icy wind is coming out of the north, the direction we are heading. We change our shifts on the oars to hourly. Two hours is far too painful on the hands and far too long to sit in the icy wind on a partially frozen moose head. We must be getting close to Dawson but I still don't recognize any of the country.

Hour after hour we row with the current through river mist until finally by mid-afternoon I begin to recognize the area, and as we float past the mouth of a small river, with a narrow dark valley laden with weather-beaten spruce winding off into hidden gold country, I realise it's the Sixty Mile River. The Sixty Mile is a river that hides unknown wealth. It has been mined along its whole twisting length right into the mountains of Alaska for over a hundred years and has made many a man rich. The narrow valley looks almost haunted. The ancient spruce on the small island at its mouth stand punch drunk after years of long, brutal, Yukon winters and relentless permafrost heave. Some are stunted to scrub, others are leaning at 45°, but all have seen a lot of men, wealthy, broken or insane, float out of the hills on the swift, turbulent waters of the Sixty Mile River.

Usually the Sixty Mile is only a couple of hours up the Yukon River from Dawson, but that is with an outboard motor, a luxury which, along with plasters, we neglected to bring on this shopping trip. However, with Gord and me rowing as if we're investment bankers working off a week of $100 lunches at the gym, we might make it to town before nightfall.

It's getting dusky and my mind is far back on the gold-laced gravel bars of the Stewart when we round the bend at Dawson. The familiar lights of town glow out of the dusk and the wind has brought the snow which is now hurtling earthward at 30°. We turn the raft towards the shore just below the old Bank of Commerce, and when it finally grinds into the gravel our relief is hard to conceal. We stagger off the raft and stretch our aching bodies as the icy wind freezes our faces. We both agree as we walk up the shore and onto Main Street like arthritic ninety-year-olds that that was one hell of a shopping trip.

WINTER 2004-5

Late November 2004

A long night

Usually we love Freeze Up. We love the isolation, the quiet, the loneliness, the freedom and the uncertainty, but this time it is different. There are people over here on our side of the river, not many but more than we are used to. They are good people and friends but it takes the edge off Freeze Up, especially as some have bush phones with internet excess and satellite TV, so we not only know what is happening in town but in the world; some are even doing their banking from home.

This Freeze Up we are not isolated – we just can't buy a fresh lettuce. This is exactly what happened to the old Sourdoughs; civilization followed them and with it came signs, laws and committees hell bent on progress – and as the saying goes, 'Ya can't stop progress!' And that's right. You can't stop people bridging rivers and pushing phone lines through the wilderness so that unprogressive people can have progressive people phoning them up during dinner to force cheap car insurance down their ear. With phone lines comes electricity which will save the unprogressive from a life of drudgery, and they can live in a push button world that will save them time and enable them to have the luxury of watching daytime soaps and re-runs of Quincy instead of listening to the songbirds or watching the sun paint another masterpiece on the wilderness canvas. Progress is obviously the way to go. Bulldoze the wilderness that is integral to everyone's soul and health, flatten it and slap up some over-priced white condos so boredom can run amok, then employ shrinks to sooth the soul and get an air conditioner for clean air – brilliant!

Thank God we have our new land up river at Bell Creek. As soon as the river is solid enough Bridge and a girlfriend break trail on the river with snow machines to Bell Creek, with the objective of putting up a wall tent for us to use as a base camp when we search for cabin logs. While they are gone Little Jack and I go Christmas tree hunting. The snow is deep and I drag Jack through the trees on a black sled as he shoots dragons hiding in the trees with the bow saw. Boris came with us but has given up and gone back to the cabin because the snow is too deep. We trudge through the snow looking at suitable trees for quite some time before we find one. It's difficult to tell what they're like until we kick the snow off them and even then they are frozen into squashed or bent positions. The temperature seems to be dropping quite quickly as we cut the tree and drag it back to the cabin to thaw out. I check the thermometer on the deck. It's -30°C and a stiff wind is blowing from Alaska. I hope Bridge is alright.

Before long darkness cloaks the forest around us and the temperature drops past -40°C. Bridge must be freezing! I pray they've managed to get the wall tent up because it takes a lot of work and is hard enough without adding these temperatures, thick gloves and darkness to it. As the evening wears on it looks like Little Jack and I will be on our own for the night. It's late and Bridge is not back, so she's probably hunkered down somewhere trying to get out of the cold.

The next morning Little Jack pulls poor Boris's long ears, laughing a wicked laugh. Boris just sits there and lets him fold his ears over his head and pull them up until he looks like a gremlin. It must be around 10.30 a.m. and the temperature is -42°C. The sun is lightening the sky behind the trees and I can just see a hint of red through the silhouetted spruce. Bridge is still not back. I'm getting a little anxious because all sorts of thing can go wrong in these temperatures. I try to keep busy and split and stack fire wood but it's too cold for Jack to be outside for long so we spend a lot of the day reading *Fat Charlie's Circus* in front of the stove.

It's getting dark when I finally give in to my fears and bundle Little Jack into all manner of hats, boots and coats to venture out to search for Bridge. We just get out of the door when Bridge drives up to the cabin and shuts off the snow machine. She looks frozen but is wearing a huge smile from behind her frosty face mask.

After warming her up with hot tea I finally get the whole story. Apparently they found Bell Creek around mid-morning yesterday and decided to cut trees for tent poles. It was then that they found they had lost their saw and had to do the felling with an axe which is considerably harder. Bridge felled a tree on to Margery, nearly breaking her arm, but they finally managed to get enough long straight poles for the tent, but by the time they had dragged them to the campsite it was dark and 'a bit nippy'. They decided to get a fire going and collect a night's supply of wood because there was no way the tent was going to go up before morning. They dug a pit in the snow, lit a huge fire and slept on a bed of spruce boughs and caribou skins under a clear cold sky with waltzing northern lights until daylight. In the morning their boots were frozen and hair frosted but it was only the extra effort it took to start the skidoos for their return journey that made them realise it was colder than when they left. I ask the most important question, is the wall tent up? It seems not. They are going to have to try again... any excuse!

December 2004

Winter Solstice, cabin fever and dreams of a big strike

It's 21 December today and this is the day we look forward to more than Christmas, for it's the darkest and longest day of the year – the Winter Solstice. From now the days stop their descent into darkness and gradually begin to get lighter and longer. It's been snowing hard the last week with lots of low cloud which has made the light terrible. When the daylight has finally appeared in a dull grey tinge around 11 o'clock, it has hung limply in the cold until 2.30 then slipped away again relatively unnoticed which makes these already short winter days somewhat hard. We really have to keep busy and make deliberate attempts to get out of the cabin because cabin fever is a real concern. Living in the darkness for eighteen hours a day, with only dim light coming from Kerosene lanterns and candles, can have a serious effect on morale.

The Sourdoughs had a real problem with cabin fever. In the early days it was common for two prospectors to join up and become partners. This was mainly done for safety but also to make their outfits (equipment) go further. The system worked remarkably well until the inevitable long winter blew in on the icy wind and the two partners would have to hole up in a tiny, rough cabin full of draughts, with each other's bad habits, and raggedy underwear drying over the stove. Long-time friendships gradually rotted away into hatred under such conditions. Usually when spring arrived it was common for partners not to have spoken to each other for months, not shared the same food, fire or water. Some did not even get out of their bunks while the other man was up. It was because of such circumstances that guns, on mutual agreement at the start of the winter, were left outside the cabin.

Many strange and interesting tales have come out of the Yukon's bush cabins each spring, some funny, some tragic; last month, for instance, in a moment of madness a miner in the goldfields killed his neighbour with a rifle because he believed he was stealing.

Over the years Bridge and I have learnt to recognize the signs of cabin fever in ourselves and each other, but even so the dark depths of winter do stir a demon that stalks the shadows of our love. Days will go by before we notice a distance between us, or the absence of a hug, the meeting of eyes or a friendly smile. Silly things will cause an outburst. Tempers are short and unpredictable and Little Jack becomes irritable and almost a nuisance. Once cabin fever starts, it's hard to stop the spiral downward to rock bottom where the chill in the cabin is several degrees colder than the winter night outside. We have found the secret is to keep busy, join forces and tackle problems together, which is somewhat difficult if cabin fever is at pot-throwing stage. But just acknowledging the problem sparks the kindling of the fire of love and slowly over the following days we swim out of the deep dark depth to the sunny surface of normal life. Fortunately there are lots of chores to do which get us outside: firewood needs to be cut, split and stacked, snow needs to be collected and melted for water, equipment mechanical or otherwise always seems to be broken and need fixing, and there are always copious amounts of snow to shovel. Now Little Jack is slightly older he is easier to get out of the door. Last winter he hated being forced into his winter gear. He would scream the place down as we struggled to squash him quickly into snowsuits and coats, two layers of gloves, two hats, a neck warmer and boots. It took so long and he struggled so much that of course he would overheat in the cabin. So once he was fully clothed we would put him in the backpack and prop him against the open door jam so the -30°C air cooled him down and he usually fell asleep. However, the -30°C air flowing over Little Jack in a veil of steam not only cooled him down but rapidly dropped the temperature in the cabin. We would struggle to get ourselves dressed and get out before the cabin froze. It was exhausting!

I've put the phial of gold flakes on top of the mantelpiece where they glitter in the light of a kerosene lantern. The sum total of our year's hard prospecting has totalled 24 cents. Some would say we wasted a year. Indeed, some have even said we are foolhardy and irresponsible to hunt for gold in the wilderness with a toddler, a short-legged dog and a staggering amount of ignorance. Many say it's pointless, a fool's errand and the height of stupidity. Twenty-four cents – you can't buy a newspaper, park your car or make a phone call with 24 cents, but to us it is a fortune. It screams promise, purpose and life. We know the gold is really out there somewhere because we now have 24 cents' worth of it glistening in the lantern light while we pour over maps of the twisted rivers and high mountain ranges where the Yukon keeps her secrets. As we trace the winding course of the Stewart River with our fingers, or look for passes in the tightly-packed contours on mountain ranges, we plan next summer's adventure with purpose and feel the future is golden all because of those 24 cents. The whole point to us – Bridget, Dorian, Jack and Boris – of searching for the Mother Lode is the challenge, the uncertainty and the feeling of truly living our dreams. An added benefit would be to find riches beyond our understanding, but we have set a realistic goal of finding enough Klondike gold to buy *Wise Mike* and sail around the world drinking tall Pimms. Any more gold than that seems to lead to all sorts of trouble.

To the faint-hearted or superstitious the Klondike gold would seem to be cursed, for it lured tens of thousands of sane men from their safe lives and thrust them into the unmapped, unforgiving wilderness of the North to drown in icy rapids, sink into the mud on the Stikene trail, freeze solid on the Mackenzie River, go blind, or die in avalanches on the Chilkoot Pass. Hundreds were lost, never heard of again. Men blew their brains out and others did it for them as they all pushed blindly north into the unknown, lured by the sparkling light of Klondike gold. The Eldorado Kings who had actually touched the elusive Klondike gold mostly died drunk or alone or penniless or abruptly at their own insane hands ... so it may well be cursed.

We, however, are not faint hearted or superstitious, just a little unhinged. To us, curses are something we shout at the dog when he's dragging his arse on the carpet. We are already mad and penniless and occasionally put too much brandy in the Christmas pudding but we are still up and digging. We are novices at the art of prospecting but then so was George Carmack, the fortunate chap who first found the gold in the Klondike and sparked the most dramatic gold rush in history.

Carmack was an ordinary fellow with a taste for salmon. He was on the Klondike River with two native friends, Skookum Jim and Tagish Charlie, to catch salmon for the winter's supply when he bumped into Robert Henderson, a long-time prospector. The four got talking, but the conversation was stilted because Robert Henderson for some reason didn't like natives. Eventually he rudely suggested to George that he should forget about fillets of fish and the two Indians and try prospecting up Rabbit Creek that led into the hills to their left. When Skookum Jim asked Henderson for a smoke, Henderson refused point blank, then poled up river shouting to George to send word to him in the next valley if he found anything in Rabbit Creek. The three were a bit peeved by Henderson's rudeness for it was odd that a long-time Sourdough would not share his tobacco, but when he disappeared round the bend in the river they forgot him and returned to fishing. After a couple of days of catching nothing but the bottom of the Klondike, George suggested a leisurely stroll up Rabbit Creek and Jim and Charlie agreed. They were half way up the deep gulch when Skookum and Charlie shot a moose – if they weren't having fish they would have a steak. They made camp and butchered the moose. After hanging the meat quarters in a nearby tree they went for a bathe in the creek and moments later realised they were standing on, literally, tons of gold. And that was it (as far as one of the stories goes), that was how the greatest gold rush in history was started. It wasn't as if a serious prospector had worked his way methodically to billions of dollars of hidden gold by mapping and tracing dispersed placer gold in the area. George sat on it while scrubbing his armpits. Henderson had suggested the creek to George on the off chance because he thought it was beneath a white man to be hanging around fishing with a bunch of Indians. If he had thought there was any gold in Rabbit Creek he would have looked himself.

The whole dramatic story gave us hope. We didn't need to be professionals, we just needed to get out there and follow the adventure. One thing that our critics should note about George Carmack's discovery is the fact that some of the Sourdoughs, the boys who had been in the Yukon for years working in the frozen mud of Forty Mile River and other unnamed creeks, didn't believe George. Even when George persuaded others to stake by showing them the gold he had just picked out of the rock in a few seconds, the old-timers didn't want to know. They had followed many a tale like George's in their time and many a time it had turned out pointless. Rabbit Creek could not possibly be gold bearing, the water flowed too quickly, so they went back to getting 10 cents a pan on the Forty Mile while Rabbit Creek was quickly staked by other less experienced men who would later re-name it Bonanza Creek and get $200 a pan (1898 dollars).

This whole incredible story demonstrates that anyone can find a fortune in the vast land of the Yukon and that no-one really knows where it is, they just know it's there somewhere. For years professional Sourdoughs had prospected the area and found gold, but nothing in the quantities that lay in the black sand on Rabbit Creek, and yet it was there for the taking, undiscovered and waiting for someone to happen upon it, which when all is said and done and proven time and again by history is the only real way you find fortunes in the frozen muskeg of remote gulches. It takes no long expensive education or degree, no real investment, no partners, no legal team and no office. It takes a pan, a shovel, half a dead pig, a few pounds of beans, a whole lot of wilderness and a whim for adventure.

Dried goods salesmen, fruit farmers, Nova Scotia fishermen, drunken Swedes, loggers from Ohio, YMCA physical instructors from Seattle were among the men frantically digging millions in gold from their claims on Bonanza during the winter of 1898, not long-time Sourdough professionals. But the richest ground in history still lay undiscovered yards away, YARDS AWAY! Five men – a twenty-nine-year-old Austrian immigrant, a railway brakeman from California, a Michigan farm boy and two weather-beaten prospectors – took a walk up a deep-cut valley draining into Rabbit Creek. In the tangle of willows, deep in the bottom of the valley, a trickle of water found its way through frozen muskeg. It looked like nothing, but on a hunch the men dipped their pan and to their astonishment, after a short swirl, had over $6 worth of gold in the bottom of it. They had no idea billions of dollars of gold lay below them and by spring they would all be multi-millionaires. It was the richest creek in the world. Each claim staked on it produced over a million dollars each and is still producing gold to this day.

I look out at the surrounding mountains most days during the winter. The snow-clad foothills roll on for untamed miles and the white mountains rise like gods into the clear winter sky. I long to be out in them searching their creeks and panning out their gravel for gold, and they beckon, even goad, me as they glow golden in the rising sun. I wish we had found a promising pan. Just a pan of 50 cents would have driven me to blaze a mark on a tree and write our names on it to confirm our stake. We could, right now, be burning our way down through the frozen muck to the pay streak which would hold enough gold that in a season or two we could buy *Wise Mike* and catch the rising tide of adventure to the sunny shores of Africa. Instead, we have a long cold winter full of planning and wondering and waiting, waiting until the water runs free once more so the no-name creeks of the Yukon can feel the steel of my gold pan. We are at the whim of an awesome land and it is truly wonderful.

December 2004

Setting up a winter camp at Bell Creek

With the temperature hovering around -20°C we're going to try to get more equipment and supplies up to Bell Creek and put up the wall tent. Having a camp already set up by the spring will be a real advantage for an early start, and while the weather is this good the travelling and hauling will be easier. We have loaded the dog sled full of sleeping bags, dry food, axes, shovels, lanterns, saws and saucepans along with monumental amounts of camping equipment we don't need, strapped it all down tightly and held it all in place with some extremely creative spidery knots. We've made a seat for Little Jack on top of the cargo just in front of the handlebars, and my position is at the back, standing on the runners just behind him so I can control the sled, tighten the knots and hang on to Jack when we go over the odd bump. The dog sled is attached to the skidoo by a dirty yellow, nylon rope with even more elaborate knots in it and Bridge is at the throttle wearing a beaver skin hat, buffalo mitts and a smile that makes me want to marry her all over again. In front of her sits Boris propped on the petrol tank and peering over the windscreen as if he's in charge. Boris is so funny, for whenever the skidoo is started he charges off, ears flapping and tail wagging, running like only short, long, fat dogs can. He obviously thinks he's a legendary breed of sled dog with proper legs, running fast and furious, but after we pass him with ease, and after a mile or so of chasing the skidoo from a long way off and us waiting for him at every turn in the river, he remembers he's pudgy, short and a trifle dim, and with that flash of reality he adds a pathetic limp to his already excessive panting. It's then that we usually let him ride up front like a figurehead carved in a force-ten gale by a cabin boy who's enjoyed too much rum. When the skidoo is stopped he springs athletically from the seat and charges off into the woods on four short but fully functional legs as if sitting on the skidoo has cured all ills.

We look like a circus act – three clowns on a train steered by a dog – as we head for the river. A cold wind is sending a fresh layer of snow across our path as we travel through the back channels and sloughs. We travel these channels because the ice there is smoother. When the river is freezing over there is little current in them so the ice forms over their surface like it does on a pond, while in the main current the ice is made up of thick icebergs that have rolled and twisted in the current for a long time until jamming on a bend somewhere. They then ride up on each other and back up like a slow-motion motorway pile-up. The resulting ice is consequently extremely rough and in places impossible to navigate.

However, it's inevitable that before long we see the eerie steam of open water hanging in the slough ahead of us and have to change direction into the pack ice. Little Jack has fallen asleep and is slipping off the sled even before we start into the jumbled ice, but Bridge accelerates anyway as if she's come to a long-awaited duel-carriageway section of the A303 late on a summer Friday evening and definitely not as if she's just come to a kilometer or more of jumbled pack ice on the Yukon River. As we fly into the ice I lean over the handlebar and hang on to Little Jack. We bounce off the first berg and Boris undertakes an involuntary Olympic freestyle dive into the snow. The second berg knocks me off my feet but I manage to hang on to the sled by the parka hood of my sleeping child who is pulled up to the handlebars and into his seat again by my action. Bridge tries for the best course through the bergs which are mostly hidden by snow, and I briefly glimpse her standing up and leaning left, pulling the sled into a turn and trying hard to keep the momentum going so we can make it through the jumble, when the sled tips over and Jack and I are flung into the snow. Luckily Bridge hears my eloquent shriek of panic and stops before the sled and our equipment are smashed to pieces. I dig down and pull Little Jack out of the snow. He is caked in snow but still fast asleep, snoring quietly. We check him over but he is obviously all right, which is quite astonishing because I have a twisted knee. We adjust the load, tighten the spidery knots once more and again head through the pack ice like a pair of Ikea shoppers with a bargain sofa on opening day. I wrestle with the sled and keep Little Jack on the cargo while Bridge steers us up over bergs and through deep-drifted snow. Boris is far behind, limping along our track with his bad leg that seems to feel better if he can cock it on every iceberg in his path. Suddenly we hit smooth shore ice and Bridge punches a gloved fist into the cold wind and yells triumphantly. We wait quite a while for Boris to finish his yoga and catch up, then we put him up front and accelerate up the winding river towards our new home.

It takes two bumpy hours before we see Bell Creek and when we do the sun crests the hills in the east and shines upon us for the first time since November. Bridge turns to me from the front of the skidoo and beams a smile that equals the sun's. We skid to a halt in the back slough which protects our land from the main river and stop the engine. Boris takes off feeling no pain and we listen to the silence of winter. The sun is lighting the snow on the trees above us and they shine with an orange glow that is reflected in our faces.

Little Jack sits by the campfire on a caribou skin, chewing moose jerky, as Bridge and I put up the wall tent. It feels great to be working together in the winter-stilled forest and we enjoy the team spirit as we cut tent poles, lash them together and suspend the heavy canvas tent from them, then cut and split enough firewood for a couple of days. The cold of night and the dark blue shadows of dusk cloak us by the time we have a fire in the stove and moose stew bubbling in the Dutch oven. Bridge and Jack read *Fat Charlie's Circus* (again) by the campfire and I put the finishing touches to the tent just as the last of the light slips out of the valley.

After Little Jack succumbs to the warmth of the tent and falls asleep, Bridge, Boris and I sit by the campfire in front of the tent eating moose and sipping fine whisky from a wooden mug. The night is cold, quiet and still. The lantern inside the tent is glowing warmly through the white canvas, the sparks from our campfire charge into the sky on haphazard, ill-fated missions to the stars, the fire's light suffuses our surroundings with a warm orange glow which holds back the dark night, and an owl screeches from somewhere in the spruce. We say little to each other, instead let our dreams wander through the dark trees around us and release our imagination to plan our new home.

It was Bridge's turn to look after the stove in the night, and because the temperature dropped she was up quite a bit, dutifully shoveling wood into it while Little Jack and I snuggled under the sleeping bags. Consequently I've had the best night's sleep I've had all winter, and as soon as it's light I get to work building a food cache while Bridge sits by the fire with sunken eyes, sipping a mug of tea cradled in her hands like a precious gem and ignoring Little Jack's requests to read *Fat Charlie's Circus*.

Once Bridge shows more vital signs and is responsive to

pinching, we snowshoe through the trees looking for cabin logs. The beauty of winter is incredible. Everything is so pure and clean and the forest secrets of last night are revealed everywhere we look. Squirrel tracks run from one tree to another. A snowshoe hare hides in a burrow in the snow oblivious to the fact that his big footprints lead to his door. A small mammal, maybe a vole, made a daring move because two neat little lines of footprints snake out from beneath a fallen spruce and end abruptly with the indentations of wing-tips and tail feathers fanned out in the snow, obviously from the owl we heard calling into the dark last night.

The silence is profound. Our every word echoes, every movement is heard. A strange feeling settles over all of us, except Boris. It's a feeling of being an uninvited stranger, almost a burglar. Life is privately going on here in this pristine natural world and has been for thousands of years but we are about to change it. We will bring, among other things, noise, gasoline, Bridget's singing, cooked meat, rubbish, plastic, radio waves, and a short-legged, long, fat dog. We will bring potatoes, bright colours, glass, child's laughter, sawdust, literature, washing up liquid and high nutrient turds. We are in fact disastrous to this small plateau which has been created slowly by millions of spring floods and carved by Yukon winds and river currents. All of a sudden the burden of our choice hits us. This is not just an ideal piece of property that we can paint, trim, or add a sunken garden to improve. This is an ecosystem that has to be altered for us to live here. We will fell homes, destroy food, offset delicate natural balances of light, dark and temperature, we will basically invade, rape and pillage, for we are the enemy. We will be living here in a world that hides from us, which is afraid of us. And because we are humans, we can't just dig a hole in the snow like the snowshoe hare and call it home. We are delicate and dainty; in this harsh environment we need constant warmth, water, food and shelter, and that's not even mentioning our desires for constant entertainment, constant comfort and constant buckets of Kentucky Fried Chicken.

Long after the sun has dipped behind the mountains we load the sled with our travelling essentials and reluctantly leave our camp and head back down river towards Dawson. Our trail has hardened overnight so the going is easier. The sled is also easier to handle because it's much lighter as we left most of the equipment in the camp at Bell Creek. Jack's seat is no longer as high and looks more comfortable with two snowshoes as side arms and it seems to work rather well. The temperature on the river is much colder than it was yesterday and the wind is bitter, making our eyes and noses run and numbing our cheeks. We have Little Jack wrapped up in a big parka with a fur hood but his cheeks are bright red and it's not long before his feet get cold. It's no wonder some of our old friends have the Child Services emergency line programmed into their speed dial. We stop and take off his boots, rub his feet until they're warm again, then put my big buffalo mitts on them. Moments later he is fast asleep and we are on the trail again.

The pack ice is looming and looks even worse than yesterday but it's probably my imagination. As Bridge negotiates the bergs and drifting snow, I hang on to sleeping Jack and keep the sled upright while we crash and bang over the ice. With each slam on the ice, Jack slips further down the sled and his legs quickly hang off one side. I lean over him and try to bring them back onto the sled in case they get hit by a big lump of ice. I yell to Bridge but she can't hear as we slam down again after another big berg. I'm barely hanging onto the sled myself but manage to grab Jack's legs and pull them up. I'm leaning over him trying to hold him on the sled when he wakes up, looks at me and bursts into tears, not because he's in danger of being crushed by the ice but because my nose is running and he has snot freezing to his forehead.

Once on the slough-ice, things calm down a little. I check the load while Bridge comforts Jack in her arms and looks at me strangely as Jack babbles on about me dribbling all over him. With the load re-tied and the wind biting through our clothes, we head through the sloughs, following the river home, and reach the cabin as the sun turns the snow-covered trees on the surrounding hills pink, and night shadows creep out of the deep gulches leading into the river.

January 2005

Putting together a dog team

It's January and it is dark, dark and cold, cold and dark – no matter how you say it there seems no end to the low of the thermometer or the night. It is supposed to be getting light earlier each day now but it doesn't feel like it. A stiff wind is howling out of the mountains, making the temperature, with wind chill, -66°C. It hasn't risen above -40°C for weeks. Life seems intangibly hard at the moment. Our wood supply is diminishing at an alarming rate and we are just keeping part of the cabin above freezing. Ice is thick on the windows, limiting what little light there is, and we are tired of it all. I truly find it hard to believe that somewhere on earth it is warm and the sun is shinning and the trees are green and people are outside with exposed skin. Getting around in these temperatures is immensely difficult, nothing works, and everything breaks except a good dog team. Unfortunately there seems to be a shortage of good dogs in the territory that people want to sell for under a tenner, but I'm still trying to put a team together.

I am walking into town this morning to try and get some supplies, and as I cut down through the trees I can feel the temperature falling further with each step. Ice fog soon shrouds the trees and hides the dancing northern lights as I walk out onto the river ice. The snow is windswept and deep, covering all but the largest bergs. When the lights of Dawson are visible through the fog I remember my nose. I haven't felt it for a while and the bridge is the only skin I have exposed so it's prone to freezing. I take my glove off to rub it and my hand instantly cramps up and the skin burns. It seems so long ago since the main problem I incurred on a shopping trip was not being able to find a parking space.

After a lonely week of walking everywhere in temperatures that could freeze dry coffee, I have through begging, borrowing, pleading and stealing finally managed to scrape together enough dogs to make a team of eight, so I hope transport from now on will be easier. We have eight of the craziest, crooked dogs in the country and it's going to be a challenge for us all to get along and to gel into a team that works. Frazer, Batman and Dingo are old friends whom I've run many times, but the rest are a right odd bunch. Boris is quite put out that there are other proper dogs in his territory. He has the memory of a goldfish, so that every time he goes out of the cabin he does a double-take, surprised to find eight proper dogs in his yard, and charges up to them barking ferociously, determined to banish them from his peeing grounds. I say ferociously, but it's just like he's auditioning for the part of Julie Andrews in a high school performance of *The Sound of Music*. The poor chap's got no style and definitely less brains than a pampered Guppy. With hackles raised, he charges into the dog yard with a sort of stiff-pronged bounce reminiscent of an overweight ballet dancer with cramp in all four limbs. The other dogs watch him for a while as if to say, 'Didn't we do this an hour ago?' Then they climb out of their dog boxes, shake the straw from their fur and bark back which sends Boris running scared for the cabin as if someone shouted 'Next!'

I am borrowing a lead dog from a friend named Sebastian. He also is an Englishman and has been in the Yukon bush for many years and meets its everyday challenges with grace, dignity and contentment. He wants to see how the dog will perform for me in my ramshackle Hillbilly team so we have agreed to go on a mush around some of the local trails in the morning. The only trouble is I've just broken the little toe on my left foot, and I hate to admit it but it's extremely painful. I can't bear anything to touch it, not even a sock. I cannot believe how debilitating it is. I can hardly walk to the outhouse. It's -30°C and not a good idea to walk around in bare feet but it's the only way I can move around and the situation is simply ridiculous.

I am making the fourteenth experimental surgical splint for my little toe, this time out of a shotgun cartridge, when Sebastian swings by the cabin around mid-morning. His dogs stop and stay perfectly straight outside the cabin as the Hillbilly Bunch (my team) and Boris greet them with an out-of-tune chorus of *A Spoonful of Sugar* which Boris starts but doesn't finish, because he suddenly sees eight new dogs in the dog yard and does another Julie Andrews impression until we drag him back into the cabin.

Sebastian's dogs are eager to get going so I gingerly put on my moccasins and hobble around hitching my team with help from Bridge. I really need Sebastian's leader whose name is Swede and is probably the biggest dog I have ever seen, so I try and act professional as I hook up the Hillbillies and Swede one by one in a fairly fluid motion. Sebastian turns his team and leaves in style as I hook up the last dog and adjust the splint on my little toe. I put on my buffalo skin gloves as the Hillbillies strain with excitement, jumping into the air barking up a storm. I put on my hat as the Hillbillies, desperate to follow Sebastian, drag the snow hook which anchors us, while the -30°C air gnaws into my broken little toe. I reach down and pull the hook from the snow, wave to Little Jack who is watching from the cabin window and hang on through a tremendously fast start until I hit the wood pile. The sled tips over, I'm knocked almost unconscious, and the main line holding the dogs and Swede breaks. The next few moments are a little hazy but Bridge runs up, swearing like a dyslexic sailor and yelling something about disasters, and grabs the remaining dogs and holds them. I come to, and she yells to me over the frenzied barks that four dogs have gone off in a huge tangle of gang line. All I can think about is the pain arcing up my leg from my ridiculous little toe to join the pain thumping out of my forehead. I right the sled and take off with the remaining Hillbillies, hoping to catch the other four dogs.

My head is throbbing and my vision is impaired as I struggle to clear the snow from my hood and face and hang on to the sled in the same manner I used to hang on to a float when I was four after accidentally kicking myself into the deep end of Dorking swimming pool.

Ten minutes later I find Sebastian who is desperately trying to hold onto the loose running dogs and his own team. I bring the Hillbillies to a halt and slam the snow hook into the hard-packed trail and hobble up to give him a hand. He can't hold the dogs and has to let them go just before I get there. I am then aware that the remaining Hillbillies and sled are charging up behind me, having pulled the hook. Before I know it the sled is whizzing past, and I run for it as fast as I can, dreading every step with my left foot. After 50 yards I lunge for the handlebars in a Will Carling sort of way and hang on as I'm dragged down the trail, my feet desperately scrambling for the runners. The four loose dogs charging down the trail in front are becoming more and more tangled, followed by myself and then Sebastian who is growing concerned about his leader. Moments later we end up in my neighbour Brent's yard and become tangled around his dogs. Thankfully he comes out to help, albeit with some colourful language about Englishmen and mad dogs. We fix the line, but as soon as we untangle the dogs and get them facing in the right direction, they take off uncontrollably. I struggle to keep the sled upright and dread the next bump on my little toe until the dogs veer off into deep snow and become stuck. Sebastian goes by with his team and waits for me further up the trail as I try to get the team back on the trail. Swede by this time is getting rather annoyed with the amateurs, looses his temper and starts a huge fight. My heart sinks as the eight dogs brawl like drunken Milwall fans. I leap off the sled and wade through the deep snow. Dragging the Hillbilly bunch apart by the scruff of the neck, I nearly faint when one stands on my toe but am woken up quickly by one biting my hand. Before I know it, the sled is rocketing up behind me and I once again find myself leaping for the handlebars and being dragged until I can haul myself up and onto the runners. We're moving, but in the wrong direction, and I've pulled my shoulder which adds to the pathetic list of failing body parts causing me pain. I hear Sebastian yelling at the top of his lungs and Swede turns and steers the dogs back onto the trail.

As we approach Sebastian and his team I try to slow the Hillbillies to straighten their harnesses, but it's impossible to stop, so I hang on and glide past a bewildered looking Sebastian. The dogs then take a trail I have never been down and things get a trifle interesting. The trail is narrow and plunges down a hillside to the river with all sorts of twists and turns. The surrounding trees laden with snow droop to three feet above the trail. My hood is whipped off by the low branches even though I'm crouched as low as I can, standing on the brake and trying to protect my little toe that is now so cold I think it could have snapped off.

For a brief moment all seems somewhat on track as I get my wind back, crouched below the handlebars and hurtling down the twisting, grown-in track with branches hitting my face and -30°C air freezing my head, but the speed is too much for one of the Hillbillies and he trips and falls and gets dragged through the snow. I slam on the brake and thrust the snow hook into the snow which brings the sled to a stop. I wait trembling on the sled, not daring to move from it in case the Hillbillies get gold fever and head for the hills. Everything feels alright and I hobble up to the poor dog and unclip him and put him in the basket just in time before the Hillbillies take off again. The dog in the basket panics and tries to jump out. I now find myself in the Yukon wilderness crouched on a dogsled bound for hell at 20 miles an hour, branches laden with snow rapping my knuckles and scraping my head, filling my face and hood with snow, while I have a sled dog I don't know in a headlock as I try desperately not to lose it out of the basket. The situation is of course absolutely hopeless and I know full well disaster is looming – I just don't know when. The dog in the basket decides it's an Olympic wrestler and wriggles out of my headlock and dives for the safety of the trail, the only trouble being that I've clipped its collar to the sled which halts its triple back flip with a jolt and the dog is again being dragged. It is then that I'm struck in the side of the face by a low branch and am felled into the snow like a heavyweight boxer in the wrong fight. Fortunately my death-grip on the sled holds and I pull the sled over with me into the deep snow. The dog (which I'm getting to know rather well) and I are unceremoniously dragged for a short distance before the Hillbillies give up and stop. I lie exhausted in the snow, wondering where my little toe has gone, when the dog clipped to the sled cocks its leg on the handlebars and splashes my face.

While hurting from the most unimaginable places on my body I unclip my slack-bladdered friend so he can run free and hopefully get lost in the wilderness. I right the sled and go hurtling down the bloody endless trail again while praying for a rabies epidemic so I have a legitimate excuse to shoot the rest of these bastards.

Eventually we hit a road and the dogs turn up hill which pleases me greatly because they slow to a walk. Three hours later we pull up to the cabin. The Hillbillies and I are exhausted. I haven't seen Sebastian for over two hours and I really am wondering what he thought of the whole episode and why in God's name I am trying mushing again.

Over the course of the next few weeks I dog mush every day and have ample opportunity to try out my ever-increasing vocabulary of obscenities and my ever-inventive first aid techniques while Boris gets a surprise every morning when he finds eight dogs in his yard. The Hillbillies themselves are like rabid Tasmanian devils until they're running, when they turn into the supreme athletes they are. Getting them into their traces is a real fight, they are so excited, and they scream and bark and jump and strain in their harnesses. It's a rush to get them underway before a fight breaks out, and I usually get bitten somewhere on my body and am hot and sweated up under my winter gear by the time I pull the hook. As soon as the dogs feel the hook loose, they charge off with immense power and acceleration, falling silent as they throw all their effort into running. If I can hang on and keep the sled upright for the first four kilometers, they slow to a pace that is manageable and I can begin to relax my death grip, stand up straight and breathe normally.

February 2005

Frozen feet at -50°C

There seems no end to the cold this year. It's mid-February and the days are getting lighter but there is still no heat in the sun. The glorious sunsets that mark the start of the cold nights begin about five o'clock with the sun turning the spruce on the hills golden. Then the clear sky slowly turns a pastel pink which fades to deep blue at the base of the horizon. The ice fog on the river glows orange and the shadows rise like a tide until the sun dips behind the mountains taking the day with it so the cold shadows can flirt with the night unhindered.

I am up in the Tombstone Mountains looking for caribou and the wind is forcing a -50°C cold into my clothes. The sun has just been stolen by the mountain to the north and the temperature instantly drops. I'm on snowshoes about five kilometers from my little cabin, the snow is deep and the going is hard which is why I take a shortcut that nearly takes my feet.

To avoid going up over a hill that is being pounded by the vicious wind I follow a creek that drops sharply into a gorge. The night is releasing constellations to shine like diamonds as I enter the gorge with its steep cliff sides. It's a narrow creek probably thirty feet across. The snow is about knee deep so it's easier going than crossing the pass. It's almost totally dark when I sink up to my knees in overflow and am shocked by the sound of running water and the pain of wet cold. My feet are wet. The cold is intense and burns into my feet. The sound of running water at -50°C is terrifying. I fight panic as I try to reach solid snow but as soon as I lift my snowshoes out of the water they ice up, freezing pounds of snow and ice to the bindings and webbing. I can hardly lift them as I slosh through a heavy soup of snow, ice and water in my search for a firm footing. I find some solid snow and climb on, but it sinks around me plunging me back into the soup. I try to retrace my steps but the snow has sunk into the running creek. My feet are numb and I know it is only minutes before they start to freeze, and the cold night now engulfing my body suddenly feels like a sealed coffin. I finally manage to find solid snow and climb out of the wet slush and begin to work my way out of the gorge and back to my trail. My snowshoes are incredibly heavy and my shins burn with the effort of walking. As soon as I reach my trail, I cut the snowshoes off my numb feet and scramble on the semi-hard trail up over the hill in the full force of the wind that sucks the last warmth out of my body. When I reach my cabin after what seems like an eternity, I fall inside. The heat shouts sanctuary and I close the door on the killer wind. Fumbling for the matches I light the lantern and turn up the wick, the light revealing the golden log walls of the cabin. I'm shaking uncontrollably and have an immense thirst. I can't get my boots off, because they're frozen, so I stand in a bowl of water, in agony, to thaw the laces and leather. When I get them off I pluck up the courage to look at my feet. I find they are still there and luckily (and I mean luckily) only the outer skin down the outside of both feet is slightly frozen and a little on the bridge of my left little toe and the outer sides of both big toes.

It takes me hours to warm up properly and I spend them huddled in a sleeping bag contemplating how lucky I am and longing for the warmth of sun. It was a close call and I could kick myself for taking a shortcut, but who would have dreamt of finding running water in temperatures that freeze eyelids shut in seconds. My thoughts race in the quiet of the cabin and I am reminded of a trapper friend who did the same thing as I have just done, only it was a lot worse and on a snow machine. It was literally two valleys north of here where he went through the ice and had to walk some 12 miles to his cabin. He made it, but his feet were deeply frozen. He thawed them just like I did in cold water and battled the immense pain for hours while trying to radio for help. No-one heard his pleas for help over the radio, and unable to walk because of the pain, he began the task of re-freezing his feet so he could walk out to the road some 27 miles away. Finally, before he re-froze his feet completely, the radio connected with a doctor 700 miles away in Watson Lake. The doctor was able to give detailed advice on how to care for his feet until daylight when a helicopter could get there and Medivac him to hospital. It was a close call and one that cost him a few toes, but because he looked after his feet the way the doctor told him to, the hospital managed to save both feet, although as he says today, 'My feet, oh, they're no good'. However, I saw his feet after he came out of hospital and sat in a wheelchair for months. They were black and rotting. So he's lucky to have feet ... and so am I.

I am in love with this world I choose to call home – the Yukon Wilderness – but I get ashamedly scared of her, for she repeatedly squashes me and preys on my weakness. She sends wind when a wind would be devastating, rain when rain would cost me dearly, snow when snow would be most damaging, and intense cold when I'm already intensely cold. She makes everything terrifying to a point where I feel extremely vulnerable and pathetic. But I am surrounded by things that stand up to her, battling with her for life and eventually winning: mountains scarred with fighting off her ice now standing proud, caribou dying from her bottomless winters and her swarms of summer mosquitoes calling the wildest land home, millions of black spruce that have emerged victorious from battling with her elements for centuries evolving into the most incredible tree. Spruce march up mountains like an invading army commanded by tall, straight generals who stand in the valley bottoms and send their troops up to high ground using creeks and gulches to eventually conquer all but the Yukon's most windswept crags. With all this valiance around me I have to battle endlessly with self-confidence, frustration and failure. I wish I could live with her like the wolves I see trotting effortlessly over the mountains, or like the raven which can function with bare feet in -50°C and thick jet-black plumage in 35°C above. I wish I could adapt like the Han Nation who found a way to live with her through generations of knowledge, but I just can't seem to.

SPRING 2005

March 2005

In the valley of the lost patrol and the white wolf

After a brutal winter that has whipped and tortured and very nearly beaten us, we can at long last feel a small amount of warmth in the sun that's shining high in the crystal-clear March sky. Everything is still frozen and motionless, only the occasional raven crosses the sky, and a transient breath of wind ruffles the frozen spruce with a creak, but there is a thin warmth in the bright sun that is duelling silently with the -30°C morning air. Although it's not enough to warm our world, it is enough to warm our spirits and float them on hidden, delicate thermals with the promise of heat and light.

The days in March are significantly longer and shrivel the nights rapidly by minutes each evening. Our world has colour again. Gone is the black and white world of the winter forests and the blurred world of the ice fog. Now the sky above is cobalt blue and seamless. Below it is a carpet of green spruce that stabs into the blue like watercolour paint on wet paper, and below the green is the white of snow still pure and still treacherous, lying like a predator waiting for any prey to venture too far or make a mistake.

Jimmy Roberts and I usually get a little restless around this time of year and go a little further afield. He says it's because he's like a frisky horse and needs to gallop to fresh pastures in spring, but if you believe the rumours he just likes to gallop, spring time or not, new pastures or not. I'm keen to see what sort of country lies up the Chandindu River which, after a winding but rapid descent through tundra and boreal forest from the mountains in the north, drains into the Yukon 12 miles down river from Dawson. It is rumoured to have gold in its heart and even a lost goldmine near its source, with caribou antlers on the sod roof of a small cabin and thick glittering veins of gold running through the bedrock below.

We have decided to head into the mountains and try to

access the Chandindu with snow machines via the Blackstone River and over the Seela Pass. I pause in thought as we study the route on the map which is flapping in the -10°C mountain breeze because this is a lonely remote route made famous by the doomed 'Lost Patrol'.

The Lost Patrol was a party of four Royal Canadian Mounted Police on dog sleds who left from the remote outpost of Fort McPherson for Dawson City, a distance of 475 miles or thirty days. It was a routine patrol undertaken each winter to deliver mail and to maintain Canada's sovereignty on the new frontier. This particular patrol was led by the seasoned inspector, Francis Fitzgerald, a short man with a thick black mustache which he groomed to two horizontal pencil points. He was extremely experienced in the ways of the North and had been a Mountie for twenty-two years. On that day in December 1910, the temperature was good in Fort McPherson at -10°C but the fog was thick coming off the Peel River, hiding mountains, sky and danger. After their goodbye waves outside the Hudson Bay store, the four Mounties mushed through the fog and into the wilderness and were never seen alive again.

Tortured diary entries left by Francis reveal that as soon as they departed, the temperature dropped to -70°C. Howling winds and deep swirling snow battered and bullied the patrol for days as they struggled to break trail and make progress down the river network leading towards Dawson. On 9 January, their nineteenth day on the trail, the Yukon finally gave them a break and the temperature rose to -12°C. They were less than half way to Dawson and only had enough food for eleven more days. Instead of turning back, they were encouraged by the warm weather and pushed on, their progress increased despite a stiff head wind. The good weather held for a couple of days and they mushed hard, desperate to make up for lost time, but they missed the vital Forest Creek which would take them south west towards Dawson. Instead they pushed on unknowingly south east and into disaster. After a couple of days heading in the wrong direction they realised they were lost and began to search for Forest Creek amongst the labyrinth of willow-choked creeks in the area, while their food supplies dwindled and the temperature again plummeted. By day twenty-six they were completely lost and down to four days' food on half rations. On 17 January Francis Fitzgerald wrote in his journal:

'....We have now only ten pounds of flour and eight pounds of bacon and some dried fish. My last hope is gone, and the only thing I can do is return and kill some dogs to feed the others and ourselves....'

This was the point Francis decided to head back to Fort McPherson after wasting nine days tramping 98 miles in a circle. The following night they killed the first dog. A fierce gale came out of the mountains and they had to batten down in what little shelter they could find. Here they ate the last of their flour and bacon to fuel their starving bodies. The temperature turned vicious on 22 January and dropped to -70°C, but still the men pushed on, weak and frozen. They found their back trail but the gale had blown it in. By this time they realised death was mushing in behind. They had been on the trail thirty-three days and now a dense ice fog plunged them into a world with no landmarks, and the river broke beneath them, plunging them into frigid water up to their waists. They made camp, tried to get warm and killed and ate another dog. Each day they struggled to keep ahead of death but both dogs and men were becoming 'noticeably weaker', their blackened skin, stretched tight over bones, constantly peeling off, as starvation, frostbite and scurvy stole their bodies while they covered less and less ground. With nothing left to eat and no dogs, the men made camp in a frosted patch of willow. They cut the rawhide bindings from the sleds and boiled them up for a meagre meal. At this camp the two younger Mounties Kinney and Taylor decided they could go no further and lay down to die. Kinney died first. Taylor crossed his dead partner's hands across his chest and put his handkerchief over Kinney's emaciated face. Taylor then lay down next to his friend and put the cold barrel of his 30.30 in his mouth and pulled the trigger. Fitzgerald and Carter stumbled on, then, succumbing to the -70°C weather and frozen limbs, they made camp only 10 miles further down the trail and lay down to die. They were 25 miles from Fort McPherson.

Feeling as if we are following ghosts, Jimmy and I skidoo through the wide mountain valley lined with tundra that the Blackstone River meanders out of to join the Peel River. The sun is high in the clear sky and the snow pure white and sparkling. We disturb a group of caribou drinking from a patch of overflow on the river. They spring up the bank and bounce through the snow with a graceful northern dance before standing to watch us with curious eyes.

Several hours later we cross the Seela Pass where the snow, sculpted by the winds, is frozen like a stormy ocean with waves breaking over one another and cascading over the contours of the Pass in amazing, static action.

After the Pass we drop down through scattered, stunted, weather-beaten spruce engrossed in an endless battle to conquer the Pass. They are the foot soldiers of their garrison and we soon find the generals standing to attention along the Chandindu River. With the sun dipping below the horizon we call it a day and make camp under a large spruce.

The next morning is as bright and clear as the day before with an early morning temperature of -15°C. We are keen to get an early start, so break camp quickly before heading along the winding path of the Chandindu River. The temperature drops sharply as we enter the shadowed, narrow valley bordered on both sides by tall mountains with rounded, treeless summits that are the trademark of the Ogilvie Mountains. Steep gulches cut into their sides are full of stubborn spruce and tangled willow, marking the sort of place where gold glitters. Along the twisting river are large trees, motionless in the shadow of winter that is kept in the valley by the mountains. Gold could very well be anywhere in the muskeg and bedrock of this desolate place. It is a long way from nowhere and difficult to reach – in winter it's an arduous skidoo ride over arctic tundra and windswept passes, and in summer the only way in is to walk for days over difficult terrain while the mosquitoes sap your blood.

I'm just thinking of a way to get in here during the summer and prospect some of the upper gulches when Jimmy stops his machine in front of me. A patch of ice looks thin so he walks out carefully to test it with his axe. The ice breaks below him and he plunges into icy water up to his waist. He curses imaginatively, climbs out and crawls on his stomach back to solid ice. He's wet but laughing and we both agree you can't gallop if you're frozen, so we make camp and light a fire so he can dry off.

It is as we are sitting around the fire, with Jimmy's underwear hanging from appropriately placed sticks, that we hear a prolonged wolf howl. Our eyes are drawn to the mountain tops. Seconds later another howl drifts over the frosted spruce. We fall silent, our flow of jokes and banter stilled, as we seek out the wolf on the mountains surrounding us. Movement catches our eye and we see him on an outcrop about half a mile away. He is large, almost completely white, and is sitting on his haunches. He throws his head back and another haunting howl hangs in the air and it's then that we see the moose.

She is lumbering down the mountain, having just emerged from a willow-filled gulch, a poor exhausted female struggling to survive the winter. Her thick winter coat has no sheen and is ruffled on the haunches by protruding pelvic bones. The white wolf glances at her briefly then howls again into the thin mountain air. We watch in amazement as two black wolves slink out of the shadows in the gulch the moose has just left and follow her effortlessly, almost casually, down the mountain. Another wolf comes over a saddle in the mountain to the right of the white wolf, and then another. It slowly dawns on us that we are witnessing the end of a hunt that has probably been going on for days, and that the white wolf is controlling the final attack. The wolves' movements are strong and deliberate. They're not running but walking, occasionally trotting. One even sits down and is groomed on the neck by another. The moose is staggering, and the further down the mountain she stumbles, the slower and more lumbering her pace becomes as she tries with exhausted limbs to wade through deepening snow. We lose sight of her when she drops into the trees, but watch, along with the big white wolf, as the pack melts into one and follows close behind on her trail. All is quiet and the big white wolf is alone on the mountain as we listen for clues as to what is happening in the shadows of the trees. We are a little concerned our presence will in some way affect the outcome of this natural drama but there is nothing we can do except sit quietly and wait. The white wolf sits on the rock for quite some time until a chorus of howls rises from the trees in the valley bottom. Only then does he leave his position and move down the mountain at an enviable pace.

When we continue our journey the next morning we follow the final tracks of the long life-and-death struggle. All around us in the snow a tragic story and a success story are written briefly. The moose tracks through the trees are weary but deliberate. She knew where she was going until a wolf's tracks come bounding in from the left. Then the moose stumbles and abruptly turns for the river but obviously slips over in the snow. Two more wolves come in behind her. A scuffle happens but she regains her feet and runs down the river pursued by four or five wolves. We lose sight of the tracks when they disappear into a dense stand of willows where several large branches have been snapped from their trunks by the moose hitting them at speed. We find the tracks in a meandering line further down the river. This time they are accompanied in the white snow by the stark red of blood splatters. The tracks become more frenzied and more snow is disturbed indicating a struggle as they lead into a stand of dark spruce. We go no further, for upon the tops of the spruce two ravens now sit waiting – the sentries of death.

We continue as quietly as we can, hoping we don't disturb what natural events are taking place in the shadow of the spruce, but we are overwhelmed by the rawness and ruthlessness of what we have witnessed. The moose was at her end having been hunted for numerous days and nights. Why she was singled out by the pack it is impossible to know – perhaps she was injured or just in the wrong place at the wrong time – and no-one would have known of her final struggle if Jimmy hadn't fallen in the river. It's a real privilege to witness the secrets of nature that occur behind these remote rounded mountains and a comfort to know that not everyone starves to death in this valley.

Two days later we are back on the Dempster Highway, having explored most of the gulches and passes in the upper Chandindu. The ice on the river had too many holes in it to get all the way to the Yukon River so we played safe and retraced our steps. We found no lost gold mine but did find some promising lonely creeks that I would love to dip my pan into, but I'll have to wait until the water is running and then maybe I'll venture back into the narrow valley of the Lost Patrol and the white wolf.

April 2005

A sudden Break Up

An April wind is blowing from the Alaskan mountains, swaying the frozen spruce, dislodging the last clumps of stubborn winter snow from their drooping, north-facing boughs. It's a warm wind and it fills the valley with life and movement. It awakens squirrels to build nurseries, causes cow moose to drive off their yearling calves so they can concentrate on their unborn, restless and heavy in their wombs. It lifts courting ravens to soar and tumble in the thin mountain air, and it brings the grizzly out after a long winter's sleep. We've been awaiting its arrival like the dramatic entrance of the lead actor in a classic play. With the days rapidly getting longer, the sun is shining from an endless blue sky, polishing, rounding and shrinking the sharp edges of winter-carved snow, setting an elegant stage for the first act in the silent but triumphant march of spring. It is a rapid march on the warm wind that unites the light and the sun to rid all but the deepest gulches of winter. It brings other players from the south, like eagles that soar on its thermals, songbirds that reclaim their old territories and serenade the early morn from tree tops, and swans that decorate the ice-covered ponds with the sort of grace only swans have as they patiently wait for the melt.

Above all it brings the melt. Ponds trapped by winter begin to soften their ice and turquoise blue water appears around the edges. During the night winter tries to claim them back by freezing a thin layer of ice over their tops, but the long days and the warm wind join forces with the heat of the sun and quickly send the cold scuttling into the ground.

Now that the wind is moving the cold out of the valleys, spring is really here. The snow on south-facing slopes vanishes overnight. Dark spruce straighten their frozen trunks and stand tall after carrying the burden of seven months of snow. Strange multi-coloured waterfowl like widgeon, pintail, eider and wood duck slip and slide on the ice as they impatiently wait for water after their journey from exotic lands. The first bear sightings spread through town in stage whispers like the winter flu. And all the time the snow is melting, melting into the moss and the muskeg, turning into dancing mountain streams and brief, low-lying ponds.

This year it seems our prayers for an early spring are working. It's mid-April, and apart from the stubborn snow in deep-shaded areas, the only sign of the brutal winter is the white river-ice snaking through the brown and budding Yukon River valley. Even the mountains are pushing up through the snow and splitting its coat. This year is unseasonably warm just as it was here in the spring of 1898 when the first miners were eager to wash their 'diggings' after their long winter's work. Their diggings, piles of frozen muck, lay above ground after being chipped out of the frozen pay streaks and hauled to the snow in buckets all winter long. Each man in that early spring of '98 wondered if he would be a millionaire from the gold locked in his diggings, or if he was bankrupt, divorced or destitute; whichever way, each pile of dirt was the beginning of a Yukon tragedy. The miners waited eagerly for the first drip of the melt and as soon as it came the water was diverted to their diggings and used to wash out the riches. Each man prayed for the sparkle of raw gold. Some planned to marry girlfriends, some to buy farms or the firm they had once worked for, others planned to get drunk, while others sweated and crossed their fingers because the water running though their winter's work would either make them or break them.

While some sluice boxes glittered with the glow of raw gold and others dulled with dirt and broken dreams, the river ice began to rise as the surrounding creeks shed their ice and poured into the Yukon River. That is what is happening this year. The main ice on the river has snapped from the banks and risen sharply in the middle, draining off the surface water into channels along the shoreline. The ice now glows greenish white in a swirling pattern as it snakes its way passed Dawson City and west towards Alaska. After a week of swinging in the hammock on the deck with Little Jack, I haven't seen the river for a while and I'm shocked by its state. Large open patches of brown foaming water have pushed ice into piles like car wrecks and more are opening up all the time. Jack and I walk up to the Look Out, an outcrop of rock that looks over the town. The Klondike is running wide open. The dark brown frothing water is flushing the big icebergs out of its valley like an over-enthusiastic spring cleaner. They are riding the fast choppy water, smashing into each other, bumping and twisting against the banks, ripping down trees and gouging out banks, but ultimately pounding into the main Yukon River ice with incredible force and piling up at the confluence. The water pushing them fans out over the surface of the main ice until it finds the side channels where it runs in two raging torrents. Little Jack and I have different ways of looking at the river. He is engrossed in the power and excitement, the noise and the action as the bergs collide into the main ice. I am frightened by the whole scene in front of me because I have to cross it; I need to get back into town to work.

We rush back to the cabin and I pack my bag before kissing

Bridge and heading down to the river with the canoe. At the river, I launch the canoe, throw my rucksack in the bow, climb in and push off from the bank into the water running along the side. It seems strange to be in the canoe again after the long winter, and after a short wobbly paddle I reach the main ice that is creaking and cracking under the pressure of the Klondike. I try to step out onto it but the ice breaks away and dark brown water boils up in its place. The ice is rotten. I paddle down stream looking for a firm landing. Eventually I find a place and gingerly step out onto it. I'm using my paddle to steady myself, so when it sinks through the ice I nearly tumble onto my face. I stare in disbelief at the bucket-sized hole the paddle has made in the ice, and I try to control my fear as I test the water's depth through the hole with the four-foot paddle. I feel nothing but the tug of the current. I think hard about my next move as I crouch low on the creaking ice, holding the red canoe with one hand as it fights the foaming brown water racing past my back. I look ahead across the 500 yards of green ice gleaming in the sun. Dawson City is right there 500 yards away. People are working, doing their shopping, checking their emails and talking about the weather, but they seem thousands of miles away to me right now. I look up river and see a huge iceberg thumping its way down the channel of water I have just crossed. It is twisting, grinding and mincing along the sides of the ice and is in a direct path to smash the canoe. Thinking: 'This is frigging typical', I brace myself and haul the canoe out of its path and onto the main ice. With the canoe out of the water and my hands firmly on its sides, I look across again to Dawson City. Five hundred yards is not that far, I say to myself, and I tighten my grip on the canoe and push it forwards towards Dawson. Halfway across I stop for a breather. The going is slow and hard work because I'm sinking into the top layer of ice and it's like trudging through a muddy ploughed field. I can hear the ice groan and sigh as I rest with my hands firmly grasping the canoe in the untested theory that if the ice breaks I can always ride it out in the canoe as long as I'm holding onto it.

The creaking and groaning gets louder so I push on.

On the other side of the main ice the water is raging past in a boiling frothing torrent, dragging ice and other debris with it as the Klondike ups the stakes minute by minute. I launch the canoe and it immediately fights the current as I try and hold it against the main ice. Icebergs bump and grind into it as I drag it up river, trying to find a sheltered area to climb in. I can't find one and the canoe is getting a pounding, so in a moment of madness I leap off the main ice and into the middle of the canoe which rocks violently but stays upright as we are washed down river. I grab the paddle and steer through the icebergs to grind the canoe into the gravel on the far bank. I've made it. Panting hard I look back and see the small figures of Bridge, Jack and Boris on the far bank. Although I'm glad to be here, my heart sinks a little, for it might be a week or so before I can cross again to see them.

The ice broke seven hours after I crossed it and now the river is filled with huge icebergs the size of large trucks smashing and grinding their way down river. It started just like it always does, only earlier than usual; with a loud crack the whole mass of ice began to slip slowly down the river like a dancer bowing artfully as she exits the stage. For hours after the main ice has been smashed, bergs, dirty with silt, gravel and mud, choke the river, dragging whole trees with them as they twist and bump, heave and fight in the current pushing on down towards the Bering Sea. Occasionally they all jam together and movement is halted. The water level rises behind them and icebergs smash banks and islands until the jam breaks and sweeps the black frothing water from below their lumbering forms to leave them shipwrecked in the gravel and broken trees.

This is what happened in the infamous spring of 1898. At 4 a.m. on 6 May the winter ice snapped and released its hold. A jam downstream swelled the river in front of Dawson and the town began to flood just as the first boat in eight months arrived amidst the thick hissing ice. The men aboard the boat were two old-timers who had wintered on the Stewart River after trudging over the ice from Lake Bennett. The town, desperate for outside news, crowded around them as the water rose, and the men described the thousands and thousands of 'stampeders' camped on the shores of Bennett waiting for the ice to break so they could race to Dawson City and the creeks lined with nuggets of gold.

The breaking up of the ice and the flowing of water has always been an exciting time in the Yukon. It not only means the long, dark winter is over and the summer days with their warm, midnight sun are here, but it also means the gold is free. Free to be discovered, panned and recovered. Free to stir adventure, make men millions, fulfill dreams and impress ladies. It is free and so are we now the water's flowing. As the last of the ice pushes silently passed Dawson, I make exciting plans to venture into the wilderness around the bend in the river where I know the glitter of gold shines from the shadows of deep gulches cut into the lonely mountains on the western horizon.

May 2005

Canoeing through the ice with Boris

During the winter I bought the hull of an old aluminum boat from a tall, butch fellow called Claire. He was a nice chap with one of those loud booming voices that frighten dogs, make men stand to attention and send ducks south. He also sold me an oily outboard engine with several sets of spare sparkplugs that he said was a great buy because it'd only been used once by his mother on a mercy mission for the Anglican Church. I didn't ask how long the mercy mission was because I was standing to attention and watching Boris quiver, but for all I knew it was for fifteen years at full throttle, on dirty fuel, over bumpy rapids, but I took it anyway because I make it a habit not to haggle with chaps called Claire.

I found the buying of a boat in winter a strange and uncertain task. For one thing I didn't know chaps were called Claire and for another there is no way I can tell if the motor runs, coughs or farts, because there has been no water around to see if the boat leaks or even floats. I have been like a Cornish kid at Christmas with a new sundial. For the past two months I have waited, with gold fever running rampant through my veins, for the water to run so I can try our new boat which we've called *Nugget*.

It's the end of May and I have finally managed to find a clear spot on the shore where there's just enough room between dirty, melting icebergs to launch *Nugget* into the hissing water of the Yukon. She floats well and looks almost beautiful as she jostles for space with the last of the passing bergs. It's only when I think about starting the engine that I realise I have no idea how to turn it on. There's no key and the tatty manual Claire's mother used is back in the cabin across the river. I try, as much as a dyslexic cartoonist can with these things, to work it out, but the realisation quickly sinks in that I will have to risk canoeing across the river for the manual or try to find Claire's mother who might, for all I know, be saving savages on another crusade for the Anglican Church. I decide it will be quicker to canoe through the last of the bergs and get the manual.

When I reach the cabin Boris lumbers down the track to greet me with his deep, throaty bark and wagging tail. Little Jack runs out in bare feet and shorts, he's so excited to see me, and just manages to shriek to Bridge that I'm home before diving into my arms and bear hugging my neck. It's a warm day, and the quiet of the spruce and the relaxed breeze that caresses the birch and coaxes out the last of their fresh green leaves, feel so peaceful and real after my time in the bustle of Dawson and the excitement of Break Up. Bridge has been working hard on the yard to rid it of post-winter drabness. Things look organized and tidy. The cabin is golden in the sunlight and, as Jack is eager to point out, the grass is green. The Hillbillies look hot and dirty and their chains grate on their wooden kennels as they stand up from their sunbathing to greet me as I walk into my home. Bridge is boiling up the last of the rotting salmon on an open fire for the Hillbillies. She looks wonderful. She has already shed the winter and is tanned, fit and vibrant. Her big brown eyes sparkle as she welcomes me home. She above all else represents home, safety and comfort to me. She is what I miss when I'm away and she is the glue and the stability in this crazy roller-coaster life we've decided to live.

I spend a great night with my family walking through the woods with Little Jack on my shoulders and roasting marshmallows over a fire, and then in the morning I walk back down to the river with the tattered outboard motor manual, Boris and a promise to bring fresh veg. At the river more ice than I would like is drifting in the swirling current, but feeling like heroes Boris and I jump into the canoe and enter the river as the sun beams down and not a breath of wind flicks the willow leaves. There is something special about canoeing on the Yukon River. The instant we leave the bank and drift through the hissing, sparkling waters of the eddies that line the worn banks, life slows, noise stops and an ancient peace cloaks us. It's a peace well appreciated and understood by the Han Nation elders who have stroked the river with their hand-hewn paddles for generations. And it's a peace long awaited and appreciated by the lonely prospector emerging from his dingy cabin in spring, when he gives genuine thanks to God that he's survived the dark winter and the water is finally running.

I paddle gently up river using eddies and backwaters and am amazed at the pace with which summer is arriving. I'm sure I can see the leaves opening on the willows which stand tall above the huge piles of muddy icebergs that drip continuously into the quiet water. Boris quickly settles in at the front of the canoe and begins to doze in the sun with his chin on the left gunwale. In the centre of the river the main current is rushing bergs, uprooted trees and other flotsam down river. When I think I'm upstream enough to push through the main current and still arrive on the other bank in Dawson, I turn the canoe and power stroke into it. Noise of rushing water hitting the canoe is the first hint that we are in the main current. I scan the swirling, brown water for a way through the debris. I see an opening in the twisting bergs and steer through. I misjudge and the canoe grinds and wobbles along the side of a berg right under Boris's nose. Suddenly Boris awakes from playing golf with Goofy or whatever he happens to be doing and leaps out of the canoe onto the berg obviously thinking we are grinding against a shore that has none of his pee on it. All I can do is shout and swear which I know he can hear but refuses to acknowledge. On the berg he cocks his leg and pees as if he's come out of the cinema after drinking too much Carlsberg during *Gandhi*. The canoe separates from the berg and I paddle forward, all the time drifting down river at 12 miles an hour. I watch as the chubby backside of my dog with one leg in the air drifts obliviously downriver to Alaska. I struggle with an onslaught of emotions from compassion to anger but give up and decide to call *National Geographic* and tell them I've found the most stupid mutt in the world. Reluctantly, I turn the canoe with the flow of the ice and paddle towards him. I jostle through the bergs not daring to look at the shore because we're being swept down river at an alarming rate. I can't believe I have to do this sort of stuff. No-one else on adventures (that I've read about) has had to chase a short-legged dog with the intelligence of a rhubarb plant down a swollen river full of debris because it's stranded on an iceberg. I finally get his limited attention with a word I cannot print here and I see some sort of response that I would like to call canine but in reality is more like paint drying on the north side of a house. I ram the bow of the canoe into the berg, and try to squash my anger and coax the stupid git into the canoe while my peripheral vision is shouting to me that cliffs are approaching. Boris begins to get into the canoe but senses he might be in trouble and skulks back onto the ice. I put on my 'Walkies!' voice and slap my thigh eagerly. This seems to encourage him but he's obviously waiting for me to turn and skip merrily down a leafy lane so he can frolic along behind.

I gingerly move off my seat at the rear of the wobbling canoe, get on to my knees and begin to work my way carefully up to the bow sweet-talking Boris like an old spinster in love with a toy poodle nestled in the crook of her arm. Just as I'm about to regain my pride and give up, Boris lollops into the canoe with a sigh and curls up in the bow. Gritting my teeth and trying not to glare at him, I gently shuffle back to my seat in the rear as the canoe wobbles and jostles with other icebergs and my only thought is that if I had a gun I am certain I would gleefully shoot him. In the nick of time I pull away from the pee-stained berg and swing the canoe towards shore. After what seems like an eternity of power paddling across rushing brown water, we grind onto shore just before the cliffs below Dawson and Boris again leaps out, desperate for a pee. I have to smile and I truly wish I was as passionate about something as he is about peeing.

May 2005

A visit from the Mother-in-law

Thunder heads boil over the horizon as Boris and I walk to *Nugget* and I question my new found career as an adventurous prospector. I am bewildered, for never before have I had to resort to words like 'sweetoms!', but my bewilderment turns into shock when I see my mother-in-law, in a waxed Barber jacket and green corduroy trousers, pulling a large black suitcase with airline tags wafting in the breeze from its handle, and she is wearing a frown that says she's just stepped in something that's come out of Boris after he's eaten rotten fish.

I knew Gay was coming, I'd just forgotten, which is a great way to start off in-law visits. It takes days in re-conditioned air to get here, and then to be left waiting at a tiny airport in the middle of nowhere by your son-in-law is the last straw. I go for the 'I'm an idiot, no excuses' routine which she agrees with far too readily. After explaining the ferry won't be put in the river for a few more days until all the ice has cleared and her options for getting to our cabin are canoe, helicopter or *Nugget*, she opts for *Nugget* because she hates helicopters and the canoe leaks. So, trying to score brownie points, I load her black suitcase into the bow and steady her as she climbs remarkably elegantly into the boat.

I watch her until she is settled in the front. Her waxed jacket against the back drop of northern spruce and muddy Yukon River makes me think life around here is going to be interesting for a week or two. She is truly British and believed it was the centre of the universe until the government banned fox hunting. She worries about things like lichen on gate posts, horses' feet, over-cooked beef and the state of manners in the W.I. It's not until I start reading Claire's mother's tatty manual on the oily boat engine I'm trying to start that she begins to worry about something serious. 'Is this a joke Dorian?' she asks in an educated English accent that bounces off the cliffs and scares the ravens from their crags. I carefully explain that the only thing I know more than she does about this boat she is sitting in is that it belonged to an Anglican.

She goes rigid and stares at the horizon as if she is having an epiphany. I go back to reading the manual. I find the start button and give it a prod with my index finger. The motor shudders slightly so I give it another and it shudders a bit more. I am looking for the choke when Gay, still rigid with eyes fixed on the horizon, asks what kind of instant coffee we keep in the cabin. I find the choke and pull it while I say, 'Maxwell House'. The motor rumbles into life and we start chugging out into the flowing ice as she states, 'I hate Maxwell House and I can't do without my milky coffee in the mornings!'

The first thing I notice about *Nugget* is that she turns sharply with a sort of tipping motion that really excites sixty-five-year-old English women and sends things lunging to one side or the other. The second is that I can't actually see where I'm going because the bow is in the air. For the whole crossing I stare blindly at my mother-in-law holding down her tweed hat and reciting the Lord's Prayer with her eyes shut as we bump into ice. It's not until we are almost across that I realise if I throw open the throttle the boat picks up speed and levels out so I can see past the bow. As the west bank nears and our short but slightly harrowing trip draws to an end, I realise something else about *Nugget* – I don't know how to turn the engine off. I'm desperately searching for the manual when we hit the bank with the sort of suddenness that brings on stiff necks and rounds off the last line of the Lord's Prayer with shrieks of 'Bloody hell fire!' As I try to help my mother-in-law off the bottom of the boat, I realise that the noise and vibrating that's compounding the problem is in fact the engine at half throttle grinding the propeller into the gravel. I drop my mother-in-law and press and pull everything that looks promising on the engine until it dies. I then realise we're being taken back out by the current, so I jump overboard to try and hold the boat which makes the whole sorry situation worse because my mother-in-law thinks I'm deserting a sinking ship and panics. When I finally get the boat tied to the shore and everything unloaded we are both visibly shaking and she's asking what sort of gin we keep in the cabin.

I leave Gay sitting on her suitcase next to the river clutching bear spray as if it's a prize-winning lottery ticket, and Boris and I jog up the hill for the truck. At least I know how to drive that – in twenty-two years I've only hit a lamp post and the same white poodle twice. When we finally reach the cabin we settle Gay down with a cup of tea and steer the conversation away from coffee and gin. Bridget is thrilled to see her mother as is little Jack, and as they sit on the deck talking and laughing. I have to admire Gay for making the effort to come and see us. It's a long way on your own to an unfamiliar country.

We actually have a great week with Gay who really enjoys Little Jack who wonders, rather loudly, why she speaks 'funny' until we explain she's all the way from England. She manages to live without milky coffee and gin but does take a while to conquer her fear of bears attacking her while she's in the outhouse. My heart goes out to her. An outhouse is not the easiest of things to deal with but must be considerably more daunting if you think you're going to get mauled by a bear while you're reading last year's *National Geographic*. She is a real breeze of Old Blighty. Our conversations at dinner are about many things: the price of petrol in the UK, Tony Blair's immigration policies, lichen on fence posts and teenage boys wearing hooded sweatshirts in public places. It is truly entertaining stuff and makes us feel somewhat homesick.

When it's time for her to leave, the ferry is in the river so crossing is less of an adventure which she is kind enough to point out. We drive her to Dawson's tiny airport and wait for the twin-engine plane to bump onto the dusty runway. We all hug each other and take photos before she walks out to the plane and climbs the steps, then turns and waves before ducking inside. I look at Bridge and see tears welling in her eyes but she's waving vigorously with pride.

SUMMER 2005

June 2005

Ghosts and mosquitoes

After Gay leaves I file off the dents in the propeller and we load *Nugget* with gold pans, shovels, camping gear, guns, food, hip-waders and long-armed rubber gloves. In short, we have everything we need to find the ancient treasure in the Yukon's lonely creeks, the only thing missing being half a dead pig and maybe the stubborn mule but we might find that as soon as we try to start *Nugget's* oily engine. The sun is shining, the breeze is warm and the water is running which all add to the fever compelling us to battle freezing water, dig frozen muskeg and sift ancient sands that just might glitter or drive us insane.

Little Jack jumps into the boat and immediately wants to go fishing. Bridge struggles to put his life jacket on as I start the engine and turn the boat against the current and up past the bend in the river towards Bell Creek and the gold-laced mountains in the west.

There are thunder heads over the mountains and they begin to hide the clear blue sky as *Nugget's* bow grinds gently onto the shore at Bell Creek. Our wall tent is still standing, but looks a little worse for wear now the snow has gone from beneath the poles which are bending with the weight of canvas because they're no longer frozen. A huge pile of bear poop is right outside the door, but otherwise base camp has survived Break Up, no flooding or ice damage is evident, no wildlife has moved in and no trees have fallen.

After we fix the tent and brew up lunch in the Kelly Kettle, we head up river to search the creeks draining in from the goldfields. A few miles up river we hit smoke swirling out of the forest to the east. A wildfire from last year, which all winter has been silently feasting on dry muskeg and spruce roots deep within the ground, has surfaced like a phoenix and flared up again to try and devour the forest. We move through the smoke and emerge into a light rain falling from the thunderclouds. Just before the next sweeping bend in the river we can see a deep cleft in the spruce-clad hills that marks the course of an in-coming creek and we decide to go and investigate. We negotiate a back slough littered with the remains of once-tall spruce that now lie below the surface, tangled, naked and waterlogged. These 'dead men' hide beneath the murky water, silently brooding, waiting to pierce boats and smash propellers in some sort of twisted revenge for their purgatorial existence in the silty back sloughs of the Yukon River.

A strong wind is blowing out of the west when we finally find a place to land and haul the gold pans and shovels up the bank. Boris immediately charges off barking at shadows and peeing on the willows that dance in the wind while we secure the boat. Hoping my granny knots will hold our lifeline, I take one last look at *Nugget* jostling in the wind against the bank before I hoist an eager Little Jack on to my shoulders and we turn into the cool of the forest to search for the creek and our fortune. Dog roses scratch at our legs as we walk under huge poplar trees which creak in the strong wind ripping through their canopies. Further into the forest the wind is confined to the tops of the trees, allowing a swarm of mosquitoes to buzz unhindered around our sweating brows.

The trees become so thick we become disorientated and have to search the limited skyline for signs of the valley cut by the creek. We have no luck and stop for a rest in the thick moss below a stand of tall spruce with ugly battle scars spiraling up their trunks, a result of freezing and splitting during the punishing winters. After a cup of tea I leave Bridge and Little Jack reading *Fat Charlie's Circus* and venture into the spruce for a scout around. Without Jack on my shoulders, pushing through the bush is a lot easier, and I make good progress because there are no bad guys to shoot and good weapons to snap from trees which ultimately end up being used on me or getting tangled in the passing brush dragging us to a halt.

I begin to see poplar trees that have been felled by beaver, their pointed stumps standing like gravestones in the moss.

I hear running water, and moments later stumble upon the elusive creak at an interesting-looking beaver dam. The creek is about twelve feet wide and slow moving with iron-stained water. Through the beaver-thinned poplar which line the banks I can see its course where it comes out of the hill and on to this flat silt build-up we have been walking on. The rock is cut deeply, sharply and aggressively. The creek was obviously once relentless and unstoppable as it dragged out the valley, snaking from the mountains and pushing dirt and minerals into the Yukon River to form this plateau that now hosts ancient poplar and winter-beaten spruce. I wash my mosquito-bitten face and neck in the icy cold water fresh from the snowcaps on the distant mountains and it feels great.

I look down stream to where the creek meanders like an old man round a bend hidden by spruce. The water is slow and the rocky bed is choked with mud and spruce needles. It is obvious this once powerful and vibrant creek has done its work and has now become weary and awaits the coming of swamp and muskeg and finally stillness.

When I retrace my steps to Bridge and Little Jack, I find them dozing in the sun, and it takes the kind of smooth talking desperate bachelors use at last orders to ladies in high heels before they consider following me to the creek. I load a sleeping Little Jack on to my back and Bridge and I push through the bush back towards the creek while we shout for Boris in the hope of making enough noise to scare away bears and maybe get him to at least come and visit us.

Little Jack wakes at the sound of running water, and excitement flits across his mosquito-bitten face. All of a sudden he's not a hot and lethargic lump of toddler in need of sugar but a great warrior on a quest to rid the earth of evil bad guys that have made the beaver dam their headquarters. He can't wait to climb from my back, strip naked and conquer the dam with his knotty willow branch. We let him go and he wades out with shrieks of delight into the slow moving creek and thrashes the jumble of logs and debris that make up the dam. Bridge is tired and just wants to sleep, so I leave her in charge of the mighty warrior and venture up the creek with shovel and pan to try and find what its lifetime's work has brought from the snowy mountains.

Above the dam the water is still and dark. Beaver trails lead off through the dense willows but I see no beaver. The brush is thick and tangled, the mosquitoes fierce, relentless and painful. It's not long before the sun is blocked out by the thick mass of spindly trees. I push through ankle-deep water and a labyrinth of spruce slowly drowning in the dammed creek. All colour and movement have gone with the light, nothing is green or vibrant. Skeletons of long-dead spruce stand like ghosts, some propped up by a dying neighbour like casualties in bloody battle, many rotting in the murky brown water, and I can't help thinking this is where Little Jack should be looking for bad guys or monsters.

Eventually I find what I'm searching for, a slow bend with a build-up of gravel that has long been covered with mud. I cut back the brush so I can at least stand upright, then thrust the shovel into the stream bed and begin the arduous process of digging down to the gravel and panning it out to see what colours are locked in its grasp.

No wind, sun or air penetrates the brush around me. I'm in a dark world riddled with mosquitoes that stab me constantly. The water is dark and stagnant in places, everything is telling me to leave and get back into the light with my wife and child, everything except the black sand glittering with minerals in my gold pan. After an hour or so of panning out the fine gravel I rest against a drowning spruce. It feels good to straighten my back and warm my hands properly after the frigid water. I feel totally alone and desperate in this dark dense bush even though my family is playing in the sunshine just down stream. At this point I can really feel how those Sourdoughs must have felt alone in a wet or frozen land that doesn't want you there. The Yukon holds many a dark secret as to what she did with lost and lonely men searching for her gold. Hundreds who have ventured north in search of a fortune to save them and their family have never returned to their loved ones or the outside.

They have been lost forever to the lifestyle, the adventure and the wonder, or have been lost forever in the icy water, the endless forests or formidable windswept mountains.

Time passes but I don't know how much. Eventually, after the 'one-last-pan fever' is cooled by aching muscles and biting mosquitoes, I clearly see no glitter in this creek and scramble back through the ghosts and into the light. I follow joyful laughter floating on the brisk sunny breeze to the beaver dam where I find Little Jack and Bridge naked as the day they were born, standing on the brow of the dam singing and playing with the sunlight cast across their tanned skin. My heart swells.

June 2005

The beckoning finger of destruction

After a night of torrential rain the river is swollen and shrouded in a thick fog that has stolen the islands and far bank. A noisy robin is chattering in the bushes behind our camp and somewhere overhead, well above the fog, we can hear a raven calling as it hastens down river.

Little Jack is crying and won't get out of bed because everything is cold and damp. In between sobs, muffled by the sleeping bags, we establish that he just wants to go home and read *Fat Charlie's Circus*. It takes a lot of promises and sweet-talking before Bridge finally coaxes him from under the sleeping bags. She sings gently as she walks to the campfire with Little Jack in crumpled *Winnie the Pooh* pyjamas clinging to her neck. His face is red, his bed hair is wafting in the morning breeze and tears are rolling down his cheeks. *Fat Charlie* is soon forgotten as he sits yawning next to the fire, wrapped in a blanket, with a cup of hot chocolate in his tiny hands.

Around mid-morning the sun finally breaks through the fog

and we can begin to see the river. We break camp, put out the fire and head up river to the creeks draining from the mountains in the west. Up river the fog has burnt off and the sun is high in the sky as we negotiate islands and back sloughs. This river is always out to hijack and scupper unsuspecting boats. We can be going along in deep water one minute and a split second later can be scraping along the bottom and busting the propeller. We try to read the murky brown water as we push against the current but it's quite an art and takes years of practice. A lot of trees, whole and in pieces, are floating on the current, some riding high like yachts while others bob just below the surface or drag along the bottom, and in places it takes some maneuvering to get through them. They must all have been floated off the banks by the rise in water level after the heavy rain last night.

We think we're in deep water when I see a twisted and battered twig no more than four inches long and arched like a bent finger sticking out of the water. At first I think nothing of it as it bobs up and down, almost beckoning us to it like an old man with candy. Then I realise it's stationary in the current. I turn and shout a warning to Bridge who's driving *Nugget* but it's too late. We slam hard into a submerged dead man imprisoned in a gravel bar and the outboard engine violently bucks and screams out of Bridge's hands as it churns into the gravel. Bridge shrieks as she struggles to comprehend what is happening and I dive for the off button and thump our panic into silence. With the engine stopped we are released from the dead man and float down stream. I look back for the finger like twig but it's nowhere to be seen. It's as if it has done its job and slipped back below the murky water to wait for the next boat to beckon over and wreck.

I haul the engine out of the water to check the propeller and find it's smashed to pieces. As the current takes us in its grasp we jump for the paddles and try to regain some control of *Nugget* and guide her to shore. Once in shallow water we moor up and begin the process of changing the propeller. We have to stand in knee-deep water as we work and it's so cold we can barely last five minutes in it. Bridge and I rotate like a professional pit crew supervised by Little Jack until the new propeller is attached to the motor. We check the engine for other damage and the hull for leaks and find none, so a short time later we are back on the river and pushing against the current again.

A huge bulbous cloud, black with storm, fills the sky, and lightening is stabbing at the mouth of the gold-laced Indian River. The Indian River curves its way into the hills and past the south side of a dome-shaped mountain whose creeks run out from the top and drain into it and into the Klondike River on the north side. It is these creeks that make up the Gold Fields and they are the richest in the world. They carry the Klondike Curse thick and deep. Billions of dollars of gold has been panned, sluiced and dredged out of their black sand in the last hundred years and rumour has it that billions of dollars are still left. But for us it's untouchable. It is left for the bold, adventurous ones who would not take no for an answer, who came to the Klondike early and staked the creeks in a gamble for wealth that has and will be paying off for generations. The Indian River is where Henderson – the old prospector who persuaded Carmack to look for gold up Rabbit Creek and initiated the major strike – spent many a lonely year sniffing out the gold. He was grubstaked by Ladue, the founder of Dawson City, to search the sharp V-shaped valleys spilling into the Indian River from the domed mountain. For years when the water flowed he travelled up and down the valleys, fighting muskeg and mosquitoes and wading into frigid water to pan gravel bars and slow-moving bends, but all he found was pain and misery while the gold, thick and heavy in the gravel below him, lay hidden for many more years to come. Eventually he decided to try the other side of the domed mountain which is when he ran into George Carmack at the mouth of the Klondike, and as history shows the gold eluded him yet again.

June 2005

Deep valleys and dead horses

The next couple of days we spend searching the creeks that drain in from the west. Nameless and lonely, they seem to have no joy on their final run to the river. After gushing down from the mountains in a fast and jubilant current that flows, clear and clean, over round, multi-coloured rocks, they unceremoniously enter the lower river valley and hit the permanently frozen silt flats that have built up near their mouth. There they are slowed and spread out over the frozen muskeg in their search for the river. Some are lucky and find unfrozen ground on their last couple of hundred feet and are able to regain some of their mountain dignity to carve a path through soft black silt and enter the river in some sort of style. A few have been dammed by beaver or completely swallowed and stilled by muskeg so no real evidence of them exists at the river. Others end up stagnating in sphagnum moss above the permafrost until the next heavy rain enables them finally to trickle, as a brown stain, into the river from below twisted willow.

The sun never shines on many creeks that we prospect. Deep-sided valleys protect and nurture ancient winter ice as if it's a priceless jewel. Dense clouds of mosquitoes hover in the shadows below the bones of drowned spruce standing motionless in the shallows of the beaver ponds. It is on one such nameless creek that I find encouraging black sand amongst the creek bed gravel. Encouraged I push on through the wet muskeg and the spruce skeletons. Bridge is feeling a little sick and gives up when it becomes impossible to keep the clouds of mosquitoes from boring into Little Jack's face, and they return to the light of the river and the sanctuary of a warm breeze. My pack is large and heavy with shovels, pans, brushes and picks. It's a real struggle to carry it through the dense mass of trashed timber. On the valley floor evidence of huge floods and ancient forest fires is everywhere although fresh spring willow growth tries hard to conceal the scars. My shins scrape against tangles of dead and broken spruce, poplar and willow as I climb over, through and between them searching for a way up the narrow valley.

As my pack snags on branches and gets stuck between trees, I can really see why the Sourdoughs used packhorses to get their equipment and supplies over the passes and into the interior of the Yukon, but as I sink up to my knees in melting muskeg and twist my ankle on hidden jagged boulders, I realise why none used them once they arrived... the packhorses were all dead.

As gold fever tightened its grip on Vancouver, Seattle and other ports in North America, horses of every description were put up for sale at astronomical prices. Many were even pulled from corrals at the glue factories and sold as fit and strong individuals then loaded, along with crates of flour, sides of bacon and dreams of wealth, onto rusting ships for the stormy journey north to Skagway, Alaska, and the start of the White Pass, one of the routes into the Yukon interior.

In the autumn of 1897, 5,000 men and 3,000 horses made their way up the White Pass, the faithful but doomed horses hobbling on sore or shoeless feet under the weight of badly-loaded packs crammed with the ton of goods each man was required, by law, to carry into the interior because no food lay beyond the coastal mountains. The White Pass which started as a wagon track through tall timber leading to the far off white mountains quickly became known as the Dead Horse Trail and it shamed and haunted all those who trudged it. After the wagon road, the trail, no more than two feet wide, climbed sharply into the foothills where jagged, ten-foot boulders and glass-like slate-rock waited to trip the loaded animals and send them hurtling down the cliffs that the trail skirted. This was Devils Hill, and it was here that men who had been storekeepers, clerks and train drivers became desperate, frustrated and murderous, and started the decent into mad, heartless beasts. Spurred on by the glitter of gold, each other and the Klondike Curse, they trudged up the miserable trail in the endless drizzle, working and beating their animals to death. If the poor horses made it past the rocks without breaking legs or cutting tendons, many sank into the mud holes and swamps that lay further on. With thousands of men and horses climbing into the mountains on the narrow trail fraught with misery, danger and death, the pace was painfully slow. Many times the line was halted for hours. The horses had to stand fully loaded, sometimes for twenty-four hours, waiting for the line to move because their owners dared not step off the trail and camp in case the line started and they could not find a break in it to enter again.

The gold blinded the men of the Dead Horse Trail, stripping them of all human dignity and self-respect. Many horses, long past retirement, physically couldn't make it and stood with weary heads held low as their owners beat, kicked and cursed them. The lucky ones died violently but quickly with broken backs and shattered skulls after slipping and falling onto the rocks 500 feet below. The ones who snapped a leg between the boulders were unloaded and pushed off the cliffs or clubbed to death with axes. It was reported by several stampeders, who swore this was the truth to their dying day, that some tortured animals committed suicide by turning and lunging off the edge of the cliffs in a bid to escape. The swamps and muskeg claimed hundreds, either disemboweling them on splintered tree stumps or trapping them midriff and damming them to a lethal onslaught of frustrated blows from their owners. Some were even swallowed whole by the swamps. Some were just left to hobble through the drizzle and campfire smoke until one of the many seeking a quick buck butchered them to sell as stew in the tented cafes along the trail.

By the time the drizzle turned to snow thousands of bloated, broken horse carcasses lay amongst discarded goods along the whole length of the Dead Horse Trail. In places the only footing through the swamps was the bodies of trapped horses, most mercifully dead but some desperately trying to die.

It was a terrible trail and only a handful of hopefuls made it to the interior before the onslaught of winter. The rest, thousands of desperate, haunted men, sick with meningitis and scurvy and dysentery, returned to the beach at Skagway to try again. There they bought more horses and waited for the winter to harden the trail and a blanket of virgin white snow to hide the thousands of dead beasts of burden that went trustingly with them into the valley and into their graves.

After panning my way up the creek I find nothing that glitters and sit exhausted on a long-dead spruce while clouds of mosquitoes buzz around my sweating face. I don't notice them. I am concerned about Bridge. She has been ill for a couple of weeks now... I think it's time to get her to a doctor.

July 2005

Alone but stalked

We drift in silence back down the river to Dawson. Little Jack dozes under the sleeping bags, Bridge sits on the bow with the sun warming her face and the light breeze swaying her long black hair, while I occasionally steer *Nugget* with a paddle to keep her in the current. My eyes scan the banks along the water's edge for suitable dead standing spruce that will be ideal for our new cabin walls. While the water is running it would be a good opportunity to fell them into the river and float them to Bell Creek where we can stockpile them until we're ready to build, hopefully before the snow flies.

Back at our cabin outside Dawson, Bridge and I have a talk on the deck as thunder rumbles through the river valley and heavy rain pounds the roof above us. Bridge promises to go to the doctor's next week but shows little concern for herself. Instead she insists I carry on alone searching for our *Wise Mike* gold because the water will stop flowing all too quickly.

'I'll be back in a week,' I say to Little Jack as he hugs me on the deck. I kiss him on his warm forehead before I put him down and watch as he skips back into the cabin singing *The Wheels on the Bus Go Round and Round* in his sweet four-year-old voice. I hug Bridge then step out into the heavy rain and walk to the river with Boris.

After bailing out an enormous amount of water from *Nugget* I start the motor and head up river through the rain which falls from dense black clouds hidden by a swirling river mist. I feel alone and strangely depressed. During weather like this I really want to be with Bridge and Jack under the cover of the deck, next to the warmth of the stove that we light when it rains. Usually we spend hours listening to the rain drumming on the roof and dripping from the trees as we read, sing and tell stories together. I can't quite comprehend why I find myself driven to be alone, chugging up a misty river in the pouring rain with a wet and miserable-looking Boris, on a quest that more often than not leads to heartache, disaster and misery.

I make camp on a small island that has been smashed by the spring break-up. It looks like a bulldozer has worked it. Moose tracks meander out of the river and along the wet sand at the edge of the island before disappearing into the shallow water between this island and a larger, more forested one. Boris has run into the willows to pee like a shy schoolboy. He's been gone for quite some time and I don't expect to see him until he smells the moose steaks cooking on the fire. I search the busted willows for dry kindling but get soaked in the process and find very little wood. It seems to take forever to get a flame from the pile of smoldering, damp wood that I would like to call a campfire.

It finally stops raining, but the wood smoke from my fire hangs around and mingles with the low, wet mist and I can't help wishing I'd brought a bottle of whisky. It's not the best idea but would probably be the only warmth I'd get tonight with no family to snuggle with. Boris will be soaking wet when he returns so he is definitely not sleeping with me.

After the rain the mosquitoes are bad, biting ankles, hands and face. I try to concentrate on cooking my evening meal but my thoughts are back at the cabin with Bridge and Little Jack who I know will be sitting on the deck next to the roaring fire reading a tattered *Fat Charlie's Circus*. I have no appetite, but force down a small meal before climbing into a wet sleeping bag on *Nugget's* deck protected from the rain by a tarpaulin. During the night I hear Boris return and whimper at the bow of the boat. He tries to get up and in but fails spectacularly before wandering back into the willows to sleep on his own.

In the morning the sun is burning away the damp river mist as I brew up coffee and feed Boris a moose steak bagel. It's early, the chill of the damp night is still lingering in the valley, the robins are still fighting in the willows and the steam is still rising from the river, but I have a warm feeling in the pit of my stomach as I study the map because my eye is drawn to a thin blue line that forks out of narrow contours in the west and falls in a straight, dramatic line to the river. The forks start high above the tree-line between two mountain tops but are quickly sandwiched between tightly-placed contours that shout darkness, adventure and gold. My gut twists and I glance up the misty river – I now have a destination.

Four or five hours later after a long and interesting search we grind into the sand below the shallow water of the creek mouth. Another thunder storm is welling up above the horizon but otherwise the day is warm and the sun bright. Boris leaps from the bow of the boat as I tie *Nugget* to the overhanging willows. After shouldering my pack I push through the initial tangle of riverside willows which, because not shaded by tall spruce, compete furiously all summer for the twenty-four-hour light which the riverbank allows. They grow thick and fast, tangled and twisted, fit and strong, only to be minced and beaten by the breaking ice in the spring. They are a true protégée of the Yukon... encouraged, then whipped and beaten, but still thriving.

The valley lives up to my expectations as I push through swampy muskeg and flood-damaged spruce at the mouth of the creek and head for the definite V carved into the mountainside. From the deep valley I can see the sun occasionally on the outer tops of the tallest spruce; otherwise it is cold, dark, damp and above all silent. The water of the creek is slow moving but clear. Spruce trees lining the banks have huge, twisted piles of logs, sticks and other debris wrapped around their trunks from violent spring floods sent from the two mountains in the west. As I push up the creek I find myself walking on a narrow valley floor that I did not expect from the map. It is perhaps 30 feet wide with the creek running on the south side. Almost vertical rocks, covered in large spruce, rise into a hidden sky from either side and a stale smell hangs in the motionless air. A well-worn game trail follows the creek, and as the mosquitoes bite my face I follow it, adding my footprints to the collection of moose, bear and wolf prints already in the mud.

The valley is amazingly still and the hammering of a woodpecker echoes loudly from further up the creek as I dip my pan into the coloured gravel of a quiet pool on a bend. It takes about fifteen minutes to swirl the first pan and I find nothing, but undaunted I move on. My next pan has fools gold glittering like Christmas lights in the dark rich sand. Again I move up the creek using the trail and stepping over huge piles of bear pooh, and then I try again. This time I'm encouraged by a thin dusting of heavy black sand mixed in the multi-coloured gravel that picks up the meagre sunlight and shines. After more than a year of searching for true golden colours in cold sands, I find it hard to look at any rock in an innocent way. Everything I see could and should be gold. The slightest discoloration might be a promise. Every bend in every stream might hold a fortune. Every crease in every outcrop of exposed bedrock might be a glory hole that might possibly have been overlooked by the army of prospectors with their crude equipment who might have trudged up this very valley 100 years ago. It doesn't even matter if someone 100 years ago found placer gold up here in a bedrock crevice or on a bend in the creek. Most of the gold will have been replenished by now, put back in virtually the same place by the on-going process of the Mother Lode weathering, which is why I know, I just know, everything I look at should and very well could be gold.

Boris curls up on the bank next to me as I dig down through a gravel pile behind a large outcrop of bedrock. He's soaking wet and panting after chasing squirrels but I'm glad of his company in this cold and lonely creek. I pan out one pan and find thick black sand but not a sparkle of raw gold. As I'm digging for my next pan-load I notice Boris has his hackles up and is watching something intently above us on the steep valley side. I look up but see nothing so continue digging out gravel from beneath the frigid water. I jump when Boris stands and aggressively barks at something hidden by the dense foliage. He doesn't charge after it so I know it's not a squirrel. I shout to him and he stops barking but shoots me a worried glance then continues to growl and woof under his breath at whatever is in the trees. The hair stands up on the back of my neck as my eyes search the dark spruce for movement. I see nothing, but I can hear movement in the undergrowth. I shout, 'Hello up there.' My voice echoes loudly against the steep valley walls but no answer comes back. I watch for a long time and see nothing, so I ignore Boris and go back to digging and washing the gravel. Boris continues to growl unnervingly into the trees and I have a real sense of being watched. When I find nothing in the pan I stand and turn. Movement to my right catches my eye. I see willow moving in the still air. Something is there. I bang my shovel against the gold pan and sing *The Wheels on the Bus Go Round and Round* at the top of my voice while Boris joins in with a volley of far more tuneful barks. A black bear 50 yards from us turns and bolts up the steep valley side through the trees. I sigh with relief and thank Boris who struts around me with hackles raised and tail erect like a prize boxer after a winning fight. I'm relieved because the bear now knows we are here and we are human, tuneless but human, and not something it can eat with ease.

I go back to panning and find more black sand so I dig deeper into the hole I'm making in the creek bed. I'm panning out a promising-looking pan when Boris growls again. Adrenaline shoots through my body and a bad feeling settles in the damp valley. I stand and again search the dark curtain of motionless spruce. Boris is agitated, his attention this time fixed on something in the valley bottom just up stream from us. I see and hear nothing. The silence is profound. I suddenly feel spooked and crouch down next to Boris and try to distract him by rubbing his head and neck. When my hand gets in the way of his intent stare, he stiffens, ducks and erupts into frenzied barking, aiming every ounce of aggression in his body at the bear which has come back and is now watching us from a tall patch of lush grass. Unnerved I shout again and bang the gold pan loudly against the shovel but this time the bear doesn't run off. Fear rises in my body. I've read about bears like this. They call them predatory bears and they are extremely dangerous. Usually they're a young sub-adult male or an injured or sick mature bear. They have little or no fear of humans and actually go out of their way to hunt us. In Alaska a young geologist was attacked by a predatory black bear. It sat on her and dragged her around for hours. It ate both her arms then buried her alive before she was finally rescued by her teammates in a helicopter.

The worst attack I have heard of was in 1999 at Liard Hot Springs, a popular tourist attraction just south of Watson Lake, Yukon. In broad daylight a 200lb black bear attacked a thirty-eight-year-old mother of two. She was walking along a trail with her thirteen-year-old son when it pounced on her out of the blue, biting her in the side of her chest, picking her up and shaking the life out of her. Her son was horrified and beat the bear with a stick until it finally backed off his mortally-wounded mother. The bear then pounced on the boy, knocking him down and biting the back of his neck before sinking its teeth into his chest and shaking him violently. A fifty-seven-year-old man, hearing the boy's cries for help, came running up and grabbed a stick and beat the bear as the screaming boy lost consciousness. The bear finally dropped the boy and retreated into the brush but seconds later charged at the man, knocking him to the ground. It sank its teeth into the man's throat and shook its head until the man's neck snapped and throat was ripped out. It then proceeded to sit on his chest and eat his thigh. Dozens of people were shouting and screaming at the bear, throwing rocks and sticks in a desperate attempt to scare it away. It finally retreated enough to enable some brave people to give first aid to the boy. The bear came back and tried to snatch the boy from the first-aiders but was kicked in the face after which it disappeared. Minutes later, as people ran for the safety of their vehicles, the bear attacked a twenty-eight-year-old man from Calgary. The man fell into the brush but managed to kick at the bear several times before it sunk its teeth into his foot, dragged him backwards and went for his neck. It pinned him to the ground, sat on his head, tore open his back and was attempting to eat his buttocks when it was shot through the head by an Alaskan from Anchorage.

These horrific incidents race through my head as I slowly bend down and pack up my equipment. I keep the claw hammer in my hand ready to use in defence as Boris and I back off down the creek towards the river. The bear watches us for a while then begins to follow. I read somewhere that the average bear attack lasts three to four hours. That's a long time to be fighting for your life or being eaten alive. A young woman attacked below our cabin in 1998 reportedly shut down and went into shock. As the bear tore flesh from her leg and backside she got bored and was literally waiting for it to finish, before it was beaten off by a hero with a stick.

I walk backwards down the valley shaking bushes and singing *The Wheels on the Bus Go Round and Round*, shouting the 'round and round' as hard as I can and it echoes throughout the cold valley. The bear hangs back about 50 yards using the willows as cover. I am spooked and shaking. All around me the valley feels wrong. It feels dangerous and evil. I never feel like this which unnerves me even more. Suddenly I hear running water, powerful running water. I look at the creek and it's slow moving. I don't remember seeing or hearing any running water in this quiet valley. Then I realise it's a wind surging down the valley from the mountains. In seconds the cold valley is full of a warm wind bending the spruce and shaking the poplar. I see the bear briefly, but movement is suddenly everywhere and I loose sight of it as aging spruce crack and fall, willows bend and shake, and heavy summer rain falls from a turbulent sky. Movement and noise is abundant. Then I see the bear escaping at a fast run up over the far side of the valley and all of a sudden I don't feel spooked in that lonely nameless valley in the middle of the mysterious North. I feel as if I'm in a crowd, a festival, perhaps Trafalgar Square on New Year's Eve. I am relieved and feel safe. In all the movement and noise I feel anonymous and inconspicuous.

As Boris and I get back to the boat the wind dies and the rain slows. I have no idea what that bear was doing – it might just have been curious or it might have been hungry. All I really know is that the timing of the storm was perfect as if it was deliberately sent to help me, so I give genuine thanks to the Yukon for the summer storm that probably saved my life.

July 2005

The unknown and the threat of winter

When I get home Bridge is waiting for me on the deck. The sun is shining and flocks of buntings are scurrying about in the long grass before rising as one and flying to the aspen trees and back again. She takes me by the hand and we walk through the tall grass studded with yellow, white and purple flowers. I know she's been to the doctor's but she seems relaxed, although I can tell she definitely has something to tell me.

As we reach a clearing in the spruce that opens up a view of the mountains she tells me that she is two months pregnant. Relief floods my body. At least she's not dying of cancer. Then shock takes over, but I'm pleased and I hug them both. This really could be a *Sound of Music* moment until Boris lollops into the picture and pukes a half-digested grayling head over the flowers.

In the evening I sit on the deck and mull over the thought of a new person in our family. The sun is burning through the thin layer of smoke that makes the distant hills blurred and blue. A pair of whiskey jacks struggle to control their newly fledged brood of four noisy and hungry chicks. The chicks are large and ungainly as they climb, shrieking and squawking, through the spindly branches of a willow bush ten feet from the deck and fight over the scraps of food their parents bring from Boris's food bowl at the door of the cabin. The squawking chicks try to fly from one branch to the next with rapid wild wing beats that turn almost frantic as they miss their mark and hang precariously onto clumps of leaves and other equally unsuitable perches.

My thoughts linger between the Yukon's moods, the burning fever of gold and the love I feel for my growing family and I wonder where life is taking us and what's around the next corner. We are, after all, in the land of the unknown where lives change forever at the turn of the weather or the thickness of ice or the amount of sparkle in the sand that lies in the sluice box at the end of a day. One thing, however, is certain: we're going to have an exciting ride because our lack of gold so far means the only place we are heading is right into another Yukon winter but this time with a new-born baby.

Africa and a tall glass of Pimms seem a long way away. We just haven't found the gold, and the salmon will be running in the river in a couple of weeks signalling the coming of autumn in the river valley. At the first hint of autumn the birch trees turn golden, which is a sure sign that winter is already galloping on a pure white steed across the desolate, northern tundra in an un-stoppable charge towards us. Sometimes we feel so far away from the outside world we actually believe we will never see our families, shiny trucks, men in suits or fast-food restaurants ever again. It takes so long to get out of here and it costs so much money that we are trapped by the very thing we love, endless, remote wilderness. And the more our family grows, the more difficult and expensive it will be to tear ourselves away from the promise, the extremes and the freedom of this land that carries dreams unbroken into daylight.

With the feeling of being trapped and the prospect of bringing a child into the world when it's -50°C I am spurred on to find the raw glitter of fortune. The end of July is fast approaching, bringing autumn and its chilling winds, frosty mornings and blowing aspen leaves. The gold lying hidden somewhere in the Yukon is, very possibly, a way out. If we find our fortune in the nameless creeks, we can escape to Mexico with the new baby until things warm up a little in March. All of a sudden the glitter of gold has more importance, more promise. We need to find it before winter once again locks it away for another eight months. Time is now short, for the nights are creeping back as winter attacks the north slopes of the mountains on the horizon with a full, unbridled charge.

I get creative and build a sluice box from an old baking tray, a piece of ribbed flexible hose and a length of aluminum guttering I found in Dawson's dump. It's not pretty and won't win any awards but I'm pleased with it. It is light and easy to backpack up the deep, willow-choked creeks and the ribbing is fine enough to catch the flour gold that always escapes. It means I can sift through a lot more gravel in a day which definitely increases the chance of finding a pay streak.

At the next opportunity I jump into *Nugget* and chug up the river through a wind that has a definite chill to it. I put the chill down to the early morning but I know it's whispering warnings of winter.

On a narrow creek near the mouth of the Sixty Mile I thrust my spade into a gravel bar and try the sluice. It works well and in a couple of hours I have a five-gallon bucket full of a sifted concentrate of fine gravel, black sand and hopefully gold that I can pan out carefully. I take a break and sit in the sun as it briefly touches the gravel bar. A nest of woodpeckers are in the trunk of a birch tree opposite and the noise the young make from the safety of their dingy hole is echoing along the quiet creek. I boil water for some tea in my Kelly Kettle, eat a cold moose steak and watch the thin wood smoke from the Kettle rise through sunbeams and spruce trees. It's all so perfect; all I need now is the gold.

It takes me another couple of hours to pan out and re-sluice the concentrates and as the last of them are taken by the current they leave nothing but sorrow. As I pack up and trudge back to the boat I work hard at damming the flow of disappointment that is draining from my body, taking with it my dreams, my will and my hope.

The sun is low in the west as I start *Nugget's* engine and make my way down river to Bell Creek where Bridge, Jack and Boris are camped. It's about two hours before I see the familiar two islands protecting our land from the main river. Campfire smoke is rising through the trees and hanging just above their frostbitten tops, a sure sign of a cold night ahead. Boris comes barking onto the beach when he hears the boat and is quickly followed by Bridge and Jack who are both wearing shining smiles which remind me that all that glitters is not gold. I relax and smile back, and a salmon breaches in the slough as it makes its way up river to spawn.

AUTUMN 2005

August 2005

Ghosts and spirit

The next few weeks I spend diligently panning and sluicing gravel from twisted, dark creeks. I follow many of them for miles out of the spruce forests and up into the mountains where the rocks are not yet rounded by their flow; where everything is brand new and starting out on the million year tumble to the river; where the creeks are barely trickles beneath tons of rock that the Yukon has chiselled from her mountain sculptures. I have followed them to hidden glaciers deep in the mountains that feed their flow and still I have not found gold; but the gold haunts me, stalks me, ridicules me, but most of all still drives me.

Along the way I have seen evidence of other men's struggle. Ancient, moss-covered shafts sunk into the frozen muskeg on slow-moving bends or floodplains. Rotting cabins long since abandoned and forgotten lurk in dark spruce groves like bad memories. Old spruce trees wear the scars of axes because adventurers, long since gone, chopped the bark and wrote their names, claiming the land beneath so they could chase the rest of what sparkled in their rusting gold pans in a desperate attempt to fill their pokes and start a new life.

These lonely relics lurking in the shadows are depressing. They show the struggle and misery men have gone through to search for their futures, but they are also heartening. They show that I'm on the right track, that gold is here and it has actually shone in the weather-beaten faces of the ghosts who once worked these old claims. It encouraged them to undertake the monumental task of burning their way down to bedrock during the wicked winters and search the frozen gravel for its glitter.

The relics show amazing promise. There is a saying, 'Gold is where you find it', meaning look where others have found it before you, but I am still cautious. The men who dug these shafts or built these cabins were not daunted by much. They were not the kind to be put off by any type of hardship or misery. They were some of the few who had actually hauled their ton of goods over the tortuous trails of '98 to reach the Klondike. They had already seen, suffered and endured hardship. What we see as monumental tasks for them are in reality like digging the garden or feeding the cat to us.

They were men like Arthur Arnold Dietz from New York City, who on hearing of gold-bottomed creeks in the Klondike, sailed north in April 1898 and found himself and his nineteen colleagues on the grey, wind-hammered shores of Yakutat Bay, Alaska, staring in disbelief at 1,500 square miles of the mighty Mallaspina glacier that coiled out of the 1,000 feet summits of the coastal mountains. This was their chosen route to the Klondike, and the ice fog and chilling air coming from it was just a hint of what lay in store. Undaunted by the unearthly view before them they loaded their tons of goods, already rusting and rotten from the leaking cargo-hold, and ventured up onto the ice and entered the terrifying world of the Mallaspina. Days later they were all suffering from snow blindness and fatigue. The constant storms that raged over the glacier prevented them putting up any tents or proper camps. The fissures and canyons in the ice forced them miles out of their way and each man sank into the depths of his own misery and exhaustion. A month later there was still no end to the glacier and they were surviving on rotting bacon, frozen beans and coffee because most of their valuable supplies had gone with the three men who had disappeared at different times into bottomless cracks in the ice. After three months they finally crossed into dense mountain forests and were free of the glare of ice. Each half-starved man hacked at miles of alder, spruce and dead fall as they dragged their remaining supplies to the headwaters of the Tanana River where they lost another man from fever.

By now it was September. The air was chilled and snow floated on bitter winds. Winter had started and they were forced into building a shelter of logs to try and survive. They huddled next to a stove for weeks at a time and argued and fought 'like a pack of animals'. The once-respectable policemen, lawyers, engineers and doctors were descending rapidly into madness as gold fever burned hot within their idle bodies. Sometime in December three of the party, unable to take it any longer, set off through the snow for Dawson and that was the last anyone ever saw of them. The rest of the group stayed by the stove fighting and crying as winter drifted snow around their pathetic cabin. All this time the gold fever somehow kept them going. It fed their will to survive and gave their eleven-month nightmare purpose and meaning. It strengthened them to dig down to the bedrock that lay beneath the cabin in the hope of finding hidden colours, but all they found was cold, dirt and disappointment, so three of the party set off to dig in the distant mountain and were killed by an avalanche.

By the time spring made travel possible the group had lost another man to scurvy and the remaining eight finally gave up the idea of reaching the Klondike. They retraced their steps through the forests until the glare of the glacier was once again their nightmare. Existing on raw beans they negotiated their way through the glacier summer melt and the network of crevasses where another man was lost. Half blind from the glare, they struggled through terrible storms down towards the distant sea. With no supplies left they started the grizzly task of killing and eating their skinny dogs which had carried their supplies since the start.

Months later seven of the twenty white-collar workers from New York eventually made it back to the beach. They were skeletal, riddled with scurvy, with long beards and toothless gaunt faces. Their clothes were in tatters and their feet almost toeless. They killed and ate the last dog before curling up in their sleeping bags to pray for rescue. Eventually they were found by a passing ship. Three were dead in their sleeping bags and four were alive, but mad and permanently blind.

Stories like this litter the rush for the Klondike in 1898 and they're all amazing. Each one illustrates that men driven by gold can and do incredible things and suffer monumental hardships and failures.

With so much disaster and tragedy on the trails it is almost impossible to believe anybody actually made it to Dawson and dug for gold; but the moss-covered shafts and rotting cabins that lurk along the deep creeks are signs that hundreds, driven by gold fever, beat unbelievable odds to arrive at the end of the rainbow.

Late July 2005

The bend and the dance of the Ninja

Towards the end of July the mosquitoes begin to disappear which makes camping at Bell Creek a lot easier. We had quite a heavy frost last night and that seems to have polished off the last of them, because as I sit by the campfire in the cool air, drinking my morning coffee, I can't see a single bug. I'm not sure if that's a good or bad thing because it certainly means the summer is drawing to a close.

A slight river mist is hanging in the slough and about thirty Canada geese are walking down the far bank. If I had my gun I would shoot a couple for dinner, as they would make a nice change from moose. Instead I watch them as they dabble in the silty water and waddle along the muddy bank. They appear unhurried and relaxed as they forage for breakfast on the waterline while the sun breaches the spruce-covered hills across the main river.

Bridge and Jack are still in the bed. I can hear them giggling so I know they' re awake, and once steam is erupting from the spout of the blackened kettle hanging over the fire I make tea and take it in to them. I mention the geese waddling in the slough and Jack immediately scrambles out of bed and runs out of the tent for a look, pulling up his *Winnie the Pooh* pyjama bottoms as he goes. I love the way he is so keen on nature and wildlife. His is a world of discovery and excitement. It takes forever to walk through the forests with him because he wants to look at everything from wasp nests, fungi and moose pooh to dead caribou, spiders and lichen. The only thing he hates is ants and that's because when he was little we put him down on an anthill by mistake and they got into his nappy and created havoc.

Today we are going back to the straight valley that the bear chased me from. I never got the chance to prospect it properly and it is calling me. It's a few weeks since I was there so hopefully that's enough time for the bear to have moved on.

The weather is warm and a slight haze of smoke lingers in the river valley as we glide to shore at the mouth of the creek. The forest looks dark and still and I can't help feeling a little nervous as we push through the willows into the quiet world of the creek. Nothing is moving as we set up camp near the shore in a spot that looks out over the river to a small island 40 feet away. Boris has gone into the bushes barking at something but I think it's a couple of poor squirrels, so we light the fire for lunch. During lunch we make up the fishing rods because last time I was here I saw a lot of grayling rising in the clear water of the creek and the hope is to catch three for supper.

Two peregrine falcons scream to each other from the cliffs above us as we hack through the dense bush to the creek. Jack is on my shoulders and Bridge is carrying the sluice, fishing rod, shovel and gold pans and complaining bitterly. Apparently the fishing rods have a mind of their own and keep snagging on the bushes. The thick brush and tightly-spaced trees make it hard to see what's ahead of us. Not wanting to run into the bear we sing songs as loudly as we can, knowing he'll be scared off if he has the misfortune to hear our singing which is echoing through the silent forest.

At the creek the grayling are rising quietly in silver rings and dart for cover as we follow the bank which is decorated with bear tracks and the occasional moose print. A slight wind is ruffling the birch trees but otherwise everything is peaceful and still. We follow the lethargic creek winding through frozen muskeg for probably half a mile before we hear running water at the point the creek takes a sudden sweeping U-bend. Above the bend the current is swift and jubilant as it falls down a slight gradient and bounces and splashes over smooth round rocks and jutting bedrock shelves. The downstream part of the bend is a 15-foot, high-cut bank with a huge pile of twisted driftwood entangled in the exposed spruce roots. Creek gravel is scattered around the spruce growing on the flat muskeg on the inside of the bend and a large gravel bar has built up at the start of the bend, all of which is evidence of powerful spring floods. The sun is dappling the greenish water and old cabin logs are scattered throughout the bend, obviously from a cabin that has been washed down stream in one of the many spring floods. The cabin logs are entangled with other driftwood on the cut bank, a few lie waterlogged in the deep pool and others are slowly being buried by the build-up of gravel, but all have axe-hewn notches gaping like the mouth of Marley's Ghost.

This corner is amazing. If any gold has come from the two mountains in the west it would definitely be trapped here. The high cut bank slows the current tremendously, taking the full force of the spring floods, and where the current first slows is always where the gold sinks. We unload our equipment and slump onto the large gravel bar lining the inside of the bend. Little Jack immediately strips off his clothes and charges, shrieking with delight and cold, into the shallow water whispering past us.

After a cup of tea we walk through the tall trees lining the banks that quickly climb to steep rocky cliffs where delicate alpine flowers cling to thin patches of soil and ravens call raucously from craggy peaks. We find an old mine shaft hidden in the trees. Alongside it two wooden buckets lie in the moss, their metal rings deteriorating faster than their cedar slats. The shaft is half full of murky water and rotting birch leaves, the cribbing logs, built to stop the slides sloughing in, curling out from the moss like the ribs of a half-buried beast.

My excitement stirs as I drop a 10-feet pole into the murky water and feel no bottom. Someone, sometime, went to a lot of effort to dig down to a pay streak that they must have believed was there.

Grayling scatter as I wade out into the creek and set up the sluice box where the water begins to slow. I choose this area because it's obvious the spring floods are dramatic here which is when most of the gold will be carried in the water. Because gold is so heavy, it drops at the point at which the water first slows, and there it lies, being slowly vibrated down through the gravel until it hits bedrock and can go no further. And it is to bedrock I now intend to go, because judging by some protruding bedrock it's probably only three or four feet below the creek bed at this early point into the bend.

After weighing the sluice down with a couple of large rocks I begin shovelling the creek bed into it as Bridge and Little Jack sing songs on the bank. I adjust the flow of water through the sluice so the gravel has time to separate properly. After each shovel-load I watch the gravel bounce and swirl down the sluice, my eye scanning the baffles, waiting for the distinctive sparkle of gold to shoot adrenaline through my body. After a couple of hours my feet are cold and my back is aching, so I lift the sluice out of the water and carefully carry it to the bank. I wash all the sediment out into a bucket and once again check the baffles – nothing. Undaunted I pan out the sediment in the bucket. Again I find nothing.

Bridge and Jack have lit a fire on the bank to cook Campbell's chicken noodle soup so, fighting frustration, I take a break and join them on the gravel bar. After we eat Little Jack is keen to try fishing, so we look for a good size grayling out of the ones rising in silver rings further down the creek. Jack is very excited and jumps up and down shouting 'There's one Dad!' every time a fish rises. I try to explain to him that we have to be quiet, but all that does is start him talking in whispers and walking like Elma Fudd hunting Wabbits until the next fish rises when he again starts shrieking with excitement. We find a large one rising in a deep pool on the opposite side of the creek and I cast, dropping the little spinner just up stream from it. We watch as the grayling darts out from behind a sunken spruce log and takes the hook firmly. I tighten the line then crouch next to Jack who is bubbling over with excitement at the twitching rod. I wind the struggling fish in and haul it on to the bank where it flaps and thrashes about until I grab hold of it, pick up a rock and kill it as quickly as I can. After a short walk up the bank we find two more, and the last one we catch I let Jack reel in, which he does in ecstatic, four-year-old fashion. At the end of our fishing expedition we have three lovely grayling for supper, but Little Jack wants to catch another one. I try to explain that we only need three, one for each of us, and that any more would be a waste. He seems to understand and tries hard not to cry but his disappointment at the fishing being over fills his bright eager eyes with tears that roll silently down his chubby cheeks.

There is no sign of the bear so I leave Bridge and Jack on the gravel bar and move my prospecting operation further up stream to the point of the gravel build-up. After setting up the sluice I again begin to shovel gravel into it and watch the black baffles eagerly. By the time I have washed the sluice several times into the bucket and found nothing in the sluice, an evening chill is in the air and Jack is becoming tired and bored. He starts to cry and wants to go and I know time is running out, so I lift one last shovel of gravel out of the water and into the sluice. I will pan the bucketful of concentrates tomorrow, as they are too heavy to carry back to camp and I definitely don't have time to pan now. I am packing up when I see it. As the last of the gravel in the sluice is taken by the current an unmistakable sparkle is left. It's about the size of a small needlehead, and excitement shoots through my body. Little Jack is desperate to go home and Bridge is calling to me to hurry, but my attention is on the little nugget shaking in the swift current of my homemade sluice box. With adrenaline pumping I carefully lift the sluice out of the water and carry it to the bank but when I kneel to look for the nugget it is gone. Bridge shouts to me that she is going to start heading back to camp. The nugget must still be there in the sluice somewhere, it's just moved. All I need is time to find it, but I can't let her go alone with Jack in case they run into the bear. Reluctantly I stash the sluice and equipment by the bank and join them in the walk back to camp. Jack is bouncing on my shoulders as he and Bridget sing *The Alphabet Song* but I don't join in. My mind is back at the creek where my sluice lies on the bank with an untouched Klondike nugget in it somewhere and a bucket full of gravel that could hold more.

At camp we resurrect the coals of the fire and cook and eat the grayling and they are delicious. It's so peaceful in this creek valley that we might be the first and only ones ever to tread on its moss but the old shaft, rotting buckets and wrecked cabin tell us otherwise. As rain clouds drift down the river stealing the blue sky, Bridge reads *Fat Charlie's Circus to Jack* until he falls asleep and I put him in the sleeping bags. He was so tired but would not let go of the day, he was having far too much fun. He now looks peaceful and contented as I lean over him and kiss his forehead before returning to Bridge by the campfire.

Bridge and I sit by the fire talking quietly and reflecting on the day's events for quite some time, and dusk is attempting to darken the midnight sun before we know it. This is our most precious time and we both really enjoy describing in detail what Jack said or what Jack did during the day. Bridge laughs hard but quietly when I tell her about the staged whispers Jack spoke in while we stalked grayling. Boris suddenly springs from his slumber next to us and barks hard at something in the bushes. The hair stands up on the back of my neck and my gut twists as I look at Bridget's wide eyes as she scans the undergrowth for the bear. I stand up, bang the kettle with a stick and shout and curse as loudly and as inventively as I can. Moments later something large and black runs off towards the creek from a willow patch 30 feet away and Boris stops barking.

It could have been a moose. It was difficult to tell, so we try to continue our relaxed talking as a light rain begins to fall, but we are both unnerved and constantly scan the bushes for any sign of bear. Sometime later we hear undergrowth cracking on the island in front of our camp and Boris again barks. This we find extremely unnerving because the island is in the main river on the opposite side of our camp from the creek, which means if it is the bear it is circling us. We quiet Boris and listen, trying to determine what is on the island and if it's the same thing that was behind us a while ago. Then a big black bear walks out of the willows lining the island and on to the shore. It sniffs the air and looks straight at us before swimming across the slough to the mainland a couple of hundred yards up stream from where we're camped. I can't know if it's the same bear that stalked me but it is definitely hanging around us and showing some of the same behaviour. We are both a little scared and contemplate moving on, but the rain is getting harder, Jack is fast asleep and there's a Klondike nugget in my sluice at the creek. I wish we'd brought a gun but a gun is a difficult thing to have around when you've got a four-year-old hell bent on shooting bad guys. We would have to keep it up high which would make it difficult or impossible to reach quickly in an emergency, rendering it useless. Instead we take the hand axe and hunting knife to bed and put Boris on guard for the night outside the tent. We lie awake for a long time listening to noises in the valley but eventually fall into an unsettled sleep.

One of the blessings of this time of year is that it's still not completely dark at night, so when Boris starts barking and I leap out of bed, which has happened a couple of times during the night, I can actually see what is out there. Both times Boris has begun to bark I have jolted awake from my fretful sleep, leapt up and charged out of the tent with axe and knife in hand like a Ninja Turtle in longjohns ready to defend my family against marauding bears but have been unable to see anything in the undergrowth. Either the bear has decided the lanky Ninja in the tent is trouble or Boris just wants to see me dance. I'm not 100 per cent sure.

When morning finally arrives it is a blessing and we relax

a little. The birds are singing, rain is dripping through the canopy of spruce, and a thick white fog muffles everything in the valley. Boris is looking wet and sorry for himself so when I light the fire he comes over to sit and steam next to it. I rub his heavy neck and thank him for a great night's work on guard duty and he grunts and huffs as he hangs his heavy head in my hand. He's so funny; despite all my warnings he gets as close to the fire as possible, and just when I think to myself the steam from his back will be smoke in a minute, he leaps up with his tail on fire.

I am keen to get back to the creek, find the nugget in the sluice and pan out the concentrates for any more. Bridge and Jack decide to stay at camp with Boris as guard. If the bear comes back Boris will hopefully give them enough warning to get to the safety of the boat. I take the splitting axe as a weapon and head back to the sweeping bend to pan out the bucketful. As I push through the silent wet forest I try not to be anxious. It's difficult to know exactly how serious a problem this bear is. Boris might well have been barking at squirrels in the night and the bear we saw on the island may be a completely different bear trying to avoid us, but then again it may not, and what was the big black thing we first glimpsed running away from camp after Boris barked? All I really know is that as I walk I can't shake the horrible feeling that I'm being followed.

I am soaking wet by the time I've pushed through the trees to the creek. The fog is eerie and thick making the bend seem haunted. It reeks of a past life, of a grave, as if all life has left it. Obviously the spring flood is when this creek celebrates life, when it is handsome and powerful, felling trees, moving gravel and roaring with vitality. That is when it is dancing in the spring festival and everybody's watching. Now, in the fog, it seems like the festival is over. The music has gone and the rubbish needs picking up. But the trees and leaves around me are dripping with rain that makes them glisten and sparkle. Everything is shining in the fog that hangs between the wet trees and swirls inches above the gurgling water, everything that is, except me. I feel alone, I feel lost and I feel a fake. I feel unnatural in this place this morning, my jacket is blue, my buckets are plastic and my shovel is steel.

I can't find the nugget in the sluice and resign myself to the depressing fact it washed out when I lifted the sluice out of the creek. As I pan out the concentrates I feel a chill in the air and my morale sinks further as I watch the gravel in the pan slowly being taken by the water to leave nothing. Frustration begins to turn to anger. I'm wasting my time. This is futile, all this effort and I'm just getting cold hands, a sore back and a deep self-loathing. But I saw gold yesterday; it was wondrous and beautiful. It had a presence that only raw untouched gold can have. And I felt that presence, it quickened my heart beat and shot adrenaline through my body, so I know it was there and I found it in this creek. But today in the dull gravel I find nothing, and all I can see is the glitter of raindrops in a haunted valley. It's as if the Yukon has brought in the rain, the fog and the feeling of misery to stop me finding it again, to distract me from my quest with strange feelings and glistening trees. I can't explain it, but I feel I should not be here sifting through the cold gravel for the glitter of gold that is, at this moment, outshone by the wet sparkling trees around me that drip flawless pearls into the creek.

It must be mid-afternoon by the time the fog lifts and the rain stops. As I sit quietly on the gravel bar on the edge of the water, gently panning, I am joined by a noisy squirrel chattering and screeching at me as it scampers up and down a split spruce that'll be felled in the next flood. With the fog gone and the sun shining through the wet birch leaves, this bend looks beautiful again. It looks peaceful and rested and it's hard to believe it was so eerie and haunted early this morning. I am still fighting frustration and the feeling of being watched but have relaxed a little and am actually enjoying being here in the peace, serenaded by the delicate song of the creek. If nothing else, the gold has given me this moment and it's worth it.

My eye is caught by a wink in the pan. I stop panning and look closer and see a fleck of gold unmistakable in the sand.

Then I see another smaller one. I swirl the pan gently and watch as the water moves the sand to reveal a third. There is gold in this creek! I'm shaking with excitement as I suck them into my sniffer bottle and carefully squeeze them into my glass phial. I hold up the phial and admire the Yukon sun reflecting on perfect Yukon gold. The flakes are truly beautiful and they do have a presence. I can feel it as I study the scars, of millions of years of travel, on their shining flanks. They are all that is Klondike, Yukon, adventure, life... and now I want more!

The Curse of the Klondike – more desperate tales

The hardships men faced on the trails to the Klondike in 1898 is nowhere better illustrated than on the route from Edmonton to Dawson City. The trail that led out of the prairie town of Edmonton wound its way north through mosquito-infested swamps that rotted feet, dark forests laced with deadfall that disembowelled pack horses, down boulder-strewn rivers that smashed boats and stole men, and over numerous mountain ranges that blocked routes and harboured murderous storms.

The trail out of Edmonton split and divided into several different routes, the shortest being 1,700 miles long. These were the longest, hardest and most dangerous of all the trails to the Klondike, yet they were advertised by the merchants of Edmonton as 'The inside track' and 'The backdoor to the Yukon'. Blatant lies about 'A good trail all the way' and 'The Klondike can be reached with horses in 90 days' were distributed freely and without conscience by Edmonton's merchants in a merciless bid to put money in their pockets. These lies cost hundreds of lives and ruined thousands more but they established Edmonton, a fact still celebrated today.

In the spring of '98 over 2,000 unsuspecting men set out for the supposed 90-day jaunt to the Klondike and less than a handful made it by the time the snow was falling in

Dawson City. Most spent two winters on the trail before finally giving up or dying. Messages like: 'Due north: Dawson City, starvation and death. Due south: home sweet home and a warm bed' and 'Hell can't be worse than this, I'll chance it' were scratched into trees along the route. They demonstrated the hardship men went through as they struggled north into endless desolate terrain that was still ruled by Indians and was virtually unknown to any sane white man. It was a terrain that only a few hardy voyagers had entered, never mind ordinary, everyday city folk wearing court shoes and top hats and expecting a slightly adventurous, three-month jaunt.

The further newly-arrived Edmonton stampeders trudged into the north, the more familiar were the marks of a stampede route they came across: endless mud, tons of discarded supplies and hundreds of rotting horse carcasses, all shrouded in silence bar the odd bronchial coughs from starving men, and low-hanging smoke from their campfires. If they managed to survive the endless forests barred with deadfall, the men had to cross raging rivers with violent rapids that capsized boats and dragged men and horses out of sight forever. By the autumn of 1898 thousands of men had become trapped in the wilderness from which there seemed to be no way out. Many tried to escape but were too sick with scurvy and malnutrition. Others halted their push north to build shabby cabins in which to rest their failing bodies, but ultimately the cabins became their tombs.

As the North became littered with dying and lost stampeders, one route became clear as the logical route to the gold. It was down the Mackenzie River system, past the Arctic Circle, across the Continental Divide and then west over the mountains and into the Yukon. It was a long hard route with hundreds of miles of rapids. Boats, the ton of supplies and the mining equipment all had to be hauled over mountains in an endless relay, through thigh-deep snow, down rock-strewn creeks and across deep, wet muskeg until winter blasted the passes with -30°C winds that brought snow and ice – and brought even the most stubborn of men to a standstill.

In the winter of '98 little shanty towns appeared in the desolate wilderness as sick men cut trees and built cabin hovels to try and live out the winter. During the dark months, when winter stole all movement and colour, teeth fell out, joints swelled, eyes sank into skulls and skin turned transparent and rubbery. But still, with little to do, they sank shafts through the frozen ground in the vain hope of finding gold. They found nothing, of course, and were rewarded with frozen body parts and dwindled rations. Cursing Edmonton, the Klondike, but never the gold, men hacked off their own frozen fingers and toes with blunt knives in an attempt to save their bodies from their own rotting flesh, but gangrene set in and competed with scurvy to kill them eventually.

These men who threw themselves with reckless, foolhardy enthusiasm at the trails that led to the Klondike were thinking of one thing and one thing alone. They could not see the raging rivers, the jagged mountains or the thousands of miles of battered forests where the trees are whipped and stunted by savage winds and killing temperatures. They were blinded by the gold. They could not feel the loneliness of the trail, the pain in their backs from heavy loads or the scurvy that slowly stole their skin. They were burning hot with a fever that could only be broken by the glitter of the Klondike. To them there was no dull cold gravel; it was all gleaming with gold. They believed nuggets the size of apples could be picked out of the beds of creeks by the thousands. Untold wealth lay up every creek, in every bedrock crease and packed between every tree root.

They were heading for the richest creeks in the world, that much was true, and the fever and the blindness were also true. But the endless, cold gravel gleaming with gold was not true, as I am finding out as I pan the last of the concentrates in the bucket. I am astonished to find not a glimmer of golden hope in the rest of the bucket. I sit for a rest and am impelled to take another look at the three flakes in my phial. Instantly my excitement is renewed, and I find myself sluicing gravel again from the U-shaped bend where the three tiny flecks came from. And as I shovel I have one thought: more gold, much more gold that must be caught in the gravel and the black sand beneath me. It has to be beneath me because raw gold is in this creek, I've seen it, it quickened my heart beat and I have some in my phial, and now it's going to get me to Africa in my fancy new yacht, *Wise Mike*.

After two days of shoveling, sluicing and panning and finding only dull gravel, I fight powerful and desperate feelings that only come when I'm alone and failing on the silent Yukon creeks, so I stop shoveling. I stop hoping. I look at myself in the reflection in the creek and see a stranger. I see a stranger making mistakes in an unfriendly world and again I feel fickle as hatred for the Yukon and the Klondike surges through my veins. I throw my shovel and it clatters noisily on the gravel bar behind me, and as I lift my head I see the sun shining through the yellowing leaves of birch trees and I'm struck by their beauty.

August 2005

Desperate times

Back at our cabin Jack plays with Boris's long floppy ears while he lies at my feet. Jack's sweet giggling mixes with the call of a whiskey jack in the humid air that has warmed the valley considerably over the last couple of days. I rock in the rocking chair on the deck looking at the distant mountains and roll my almost empty phial of gold back and forth between my thumb and index finger while I dwell on the cruelty that comes with a glint of gold and fair-weather promise of riches.

Bridge is beginning to get a bump. She's looking quite beautiful, natural and womanly, quite a contrast from the rebellious teenager I met eighteen years ago. She was lovely then but a long way from the inspiration she is today. As I rub the phial of gold in my hand I have a heavy feeling. I hope with all my heart that I'm not letting her down.

With the bump now showing and winter moving in fast, a sense of urgency is in the air and growing all the time. We need the gold to give us money to get out of this wilderness for a couple of months after the baby is born, but I can't help thinking how ironic everything is. We started looking for Klondike gold for the sense of adventure, for experiences and for fun and we have certainly had a lot, but now we actually need it. Like a drug the gold has worked its way under our skin so that it seems we can do nothing without it. Every plan we have for the future needs gold to fuel it. We are tortured daily by the Yukon and her elusive gold, we can't see past the gold and see no beauty in her. Instead, every once-beautiful mountain we look at makes us wonder if gold is within, every once-beautiful creek we walk up we wonder if it might hold more than grayling, and every once-beautiful rock we touch we wonder if it has the glitter we are searching for. It's sad because we know she is beautiful and hope one day she will be again to us. But for now her timeless beauty is shadowed by the raw gold that is never in the mountains, creeks or rocks that we search.

As we know that gold is heavy and has to be lying somewhere at the bottom, it's from there that it fuels our dreams and gives us hope. The gold is always at the bottom of the gravel in the creeks – until we have dug down for it. It is always in the bottom of the pan – until we have carefully panned all the sand back into the creek and the pan is empty. The bucket full of concentrated gravel sluiced from the creek beds always has gold in the bottom – until we've sieved every last painful grain of sand in it. And when we find nothing in the bottom of the bucket we know there is gold lying in wait at the bottom of the next creek, we just know it.

As history shows, the nature of gold is elusive and the only thing guaranteed is that it's at the bottom somewhere and could be a few feet from where we've been digging and found nothing. Even on Bonanza and Eldorado, some men lucky enough to have staked a claim dug to the bottom and found nothing as they watched their neighbours, only feet away, haul millions of dollars from the bottom of their claims. This was, and still is commonplace and makes you realise why men are driven insane. The Yukon makes you work extremely hard for everything and she may decide to reward you, but she'll wait until you've finished the job and you're exhausted to let you know whether it's time to celebrate, to move on, or to put a bullet through your skull, but one way or another you'll know when you've reached the bottom.

I am struggling with motivation. We really need to find gold before winter sets in but I am tired of digging gravel, tired of searching dark gulches, tired of myself and tired of finding nothing in everything. Bridge has just brought the winter clothes out from the shed and hung them up in the cabin. The familiar, bulky parkas, gloves and heavy boots are filled with memories and moths but hang in the cabin like Mafia hit men waiting for their moment. When do we stop following dreams and chasing rainbows? There seems no reward in it now the baby is coming and winter is riding in.

I force myself to look again for gold in hidden gulches. It's raining, the air is full of smoke and I'm alone. Bridge and Little Jack are staying behind in the cabin and Boris refused to come with me, so I'm feeling a fool like most people do when even their dog deserts them. I've brought the gun because if I don't find gold I might find an unlucky moose which will at least make the journey worth something.

As I chug up the river in *Nugget* I am drawn once more into the timeless endlessness of the remote Yukon wilderness. Because the distant mountains are now deep in winter their streams are frozen which has dropped the water in the Yukon River considerably. The sand bars are visible and the dead men stick out. Bald eagles are congregating on the river and sit like emperors in the golden birch or fight like beggars over a rotting salmon carcass on the sands. Scribbley Vs of sandhill cranes, whose lofty bickering fills the smoky wet sky, are fleeing south before frozen tundra and dead salmon. I wish I could join them. The cranes fly effortlessly high above troubles and problems. I wish Bridge, Little Jack and I could just up and fly south for the winter. I really wish.

Darkness looms out of the rain before I'm ready for it. After a summer of constant daylight, it takes a lot to get used to the fact that darkness is coming and I'm caught off guard like the fathead I am. I struggle to find a place to land the boat and camp. The darkness seems to accelerate like a boy racer at a red light once I notice it and I really have to study the river and the banks to find a suitable site.

Once I shut off *Nugget's* engine I am thrust into a wet, silent, dark world. As I step on to the soaked beach rain is hitting my face, dripping down my neck and trickling down my back to the wet sand below me, taking with it my soul. Dark has taken the woods but I can hear the rain hitting the trees somewhere in the gloom and I think about lighting a fire for some kind of comfort, but last year's batteries in my torch are pushing out a weak, orange glow so searching for firewood might be a tad tricky. Instead I decide to pitch the tent and dive into a John Grisham novel while the dim torchlight lasts. As I put up the tent in the dark the rain is hitting it with a vengeance and I just know that it's filling with water but I struggle on, and for what little comfort I can derive from the situation, I repeat the words 'At least it's not windy' over and over again into the gloom around me. It's then that the wind picks up.

Before I know it the cold rain has moved from hitting the top of my head to hitting my right cheek and is now sailing past me on an Arctic wind from the northern tundra. My wet fingers become incredibly cold as I finally secure the fly sheet. I am soaked to the skin as I run back to the boat and tie her up properly to a dead man locked into the beach. Then I grab my sleeping bag which acts like a pissed-off python in the wind and stumble over obstacles on the beach that I have not noticed before and dive into the tent only to land in a pool of cold water that quickly soaks into my sleeping bag. I try to ignore the wet and cold and read my John Grisham novel in the dull light of the torch as the side of the tent is blown nosily into my face and cold water drips onto my already wet sleeping bag. The novel is about hot cotton fields, painted houses and fresh vegetables. I throw it at my feet, vowing to light the fire with it in the morning and then switch off the torch – hot cotton fields, fresh vegetables and painted houses!

Sometime in the night the wind and rain pass out of the valley like a bachelor party leaving a bar. Everything goes quiet, the tent stops acting like a flamenco dancer and the drip from the canvas turns into a droplet and I become aware of cold, a damp cold, a freezing cold. Then I realise the droplet hanging from the tent roof above me is frozen. I put my parka on and that is wet and partly frozen too.

When daylight throws contorted shadows onto my cold world inside the tent I begin the mental challenge of getting out of bed, a challenge made harder now I can see my breath. After I give myself a really stiff talking-to, I emerge from the tent into a frozen foggy day. Frost is hanging from the willows that stand motionless in the grey fog. Ice is in the puddles, the sand is frozen and a chill is taking my fingers and toes and tickling my nose. I want to go home. I want to go home and fight dragons with little Jack. I want to sit by the stove and think up baby names with Bridge over a cup of tea. I want to laugh at Boris insisting on the best place next to the stove. I want to laugh. I want to go home.

After dragging driftwood into a pile I manage to get a campfire going and the wood smoke lingers in the willows, unable to climb into the air because of the low pressure in the valley. I study the map and wait for the coffee hanging over the fire to percolate. I am trying to get my pen to write when I hear a serious commotion in the frosted willows behind me. I turn to see a whiskey jack bursting out of the silver-coated willows followed by the menacing shape of a goshawk, which in turn is followed by another shrieking whiskey jack.

The first whiskey jack sees me and banks away and, with a flick of its tail, the goshawk follows. A puff of grey feathers explodes into the air as the hawk sinks its talons into the body of its panicking prey and they both fall on to the frozen sand yards from where I sit. A split second later the second whiskey jack lands on a nearby willow shrieking and squawking at the hawk who has now pinned its struggling and shrieking prey onto the sand and is violently plucking feathers from its breast with its hooked beak. I dare not move as I watch the hawk rip feathers then gouge chunks of flesh from the whiskey jack's breast as the other whiskey jack, obviously its mate, tries in vain to drive the hawk away with swoops, dives and haunting shrieks. The pinned whiskey jack's shrieks turn to dull gurgles and wheezes as more flesh is ripped from its body and its life fades away.

I don't see what happens next because the hawk drops its wings to hide its victim but I do see it dip its head and a brief one-sided struggle occur, then the hawk flaps on the gravel, scattering the plucked breast feathers of its prey and is air born, flying into the fog with the lifeless body of the whiskey jack hanging between its talons. The second whiskey jack follows quickly with rapid wing beats, squawking and shrieking in a desperate but futile attempt to rescue its mate from the talons of the raptor. I watch them go into the fog and listen as the pursuing whiskey jack's frantic screams fade to nothing in the distance in the forests of the far bank.

I am alone again in the fog-blurred world of my camp. As the river gurgles and the fire cracks, I sit in shock studying the delicate breast feathers scattered on the hard sand, the only evidence of what has just happened. I have just witnessed at close quarters a sudden, violent event that took a life, broke a bond and secured a future, and I really have to fight not to judge, criticize, hate or admire, but it really brings my own woes into perspective. A chill runs down my spine as I stand up to rescue the coffee bubbling in the pot, but I move with confidence and concentrate on the task at hand knowing full well nothing is going to suddenly swoop out of the sky, drag me to the ground and tear flesh from my body.

When the fog rises enough I break camp and meander down the gurgling river towards the Stewart River, stopping occasionally to investigate creeks trickling out of dark forested gulches carved into the hills. I find a fleck of gold in the mouth of one creek but not enough to spark a great deal of interest. It's rewarding so I put it in my phial and walk further up the creek. The birch leaves are golden and raining down past silver trunks to the frosted valley floor as I walk along the bank. I find a perfect place to dig. The water is slow and drops a few inches to a sweeping gravel bar that naturally sifts its sands. I sit by the water and try to summon the will to thrust my spade in and dig. Dig to the gold, to *Wise Mike* gold and to Africa and a tall glass of Pimms. But all I see is a sore back, dull gravel, a wasted day and winter falling in over the pass when I still have no meat and little firewood. But I do ... I dig.

My coffee is a long time stale above cooling embers of the fire on the bank when I finally begin to pan out the fines of sand I've managed to sluice from the gravel. As the black sand is swirled gently out of the pan it leaves gold. Not a lot, but it leaves gold, seven small flakes in the bottom of my rusty pan shining like new-born children. They bring a smile to my face but a dull to my heart. I must be 90 miles up river, a long way from home. I could stake a claim here and I would find more gold, but would it be worth doing? How often would I manage to get here? And would it get us out of the Yukon before January?

I walk back to the boat at the mouth of the creek. I have a strange feeling which I haven't been able to shift after watching the goshawk tear flesh from the struggling whiskey jack as its mate shrieked in desperation from the willows: I have a great life. Bridget's and my dreams are fulfilled beyond our expectations. We have a beautiful home, a lovely son and a short dog. We feel safe and happy, opportunity and adventure is everywhere for us ... but ... but the gold sits in the creeks waiting to be discovered and its shine darkens our path. I'm not sure which way to go any more and it feels like I'm wasting my time dragging Bridge and Little Jack and the unborn baby into a winter we are far from prepared for. I'm a little unnerved, and I believe, really believe, that I should give up the search for gold before the Klondike Curse bursts out of the willows at me.

I camp the night at the mouth of the creek and cook Campbell's chicken noodle soup in my gold pan over the fire while the running water serenades me. The dark spruce forest is behind me and the silent river is just beyond my fire. A chill is in the air and pokes me in the back as I sit and listen to an owl hooting in the spruce. The sky is clear and the constellations are out and bright. Orion the Hunter is back stalking the night skies after a summer of no shadows and he looks magnificent as the northern lights waltz out of the horizon to flirt and dance with him in the silence. Tonight everything is ... unfortunately perfect. Everything tonight is pure Yukon, pure Klondike. Tonight stirs thoughts of gold, adventure and life, and a sinking feeling sits in my stomach as I realise that I'm not sure I can give up my search.

In the morning the fog is back and swirling inches from the hissing river. I break camp and drift down the river with a hot cup of coffee as the fog dampens my clothing. I see a gaggle of Canada geese at the entrance to a back slough. There are probably thirty and I quietly reach for my gun. As I look through the sights I am aware of something looking back and I raise my head to see a small bull moose watching me from the bank. I have to look twice through the fog but it's definitely a small moose with spiky antlers. My pulse quickens as I realise my winter meat is watching me from the bank as I drift quietly passed, even though I can barely see the black of its body 30 yards away in the fog. I wait until I'm slightly past so I can shoot into the side of its chest and kill it cleanly, and I'm just about to pull the trigger when movement to my left draws my attention. It's a female moose calling softly and walking nervously on to the beach towards the small moose that I have in my sights. She is slightly larger than the male and is obviously its mother. I think twice as the silent current takes me past. I should really shoot the young bull. It would be good meat and enough to last my family six months. But as it stands naively watching me, with its mother walking nervously towards it, I feel like a goshawk. I lower my gun, and as I put on the safety, I whisper, 'Winter's coming – good luck!' into the fog. Moments later they disappear into the gloom and I wonder if they were ever there.

As I drift quietly on, with spruce-covered islands looming into view then drifting away again, I decide over the mug of now-cold black coffee that the Yukon has beaten me. She will keep her secrets. I don't want the Curse of the Klondike. My life is too good. I can stay in my cabin and enjoy life with my family. I can be me and enjoy the wilds, play dragons with Jack, laugh with Bridge and occasionally curse Boris for dragging his arse on the carpet. I don't need the anguish and heartache of digging down to the bottom through frozen ground to raw gold. That is for hardier men than I am. I just don't need it. What I do need is to take my family out of the brutal winter in January and maybe not to Africa and tall Pimms but just out of the -50°C darkness, and Klondike gold is not going to do that. I've resigned myself to that. I'll just have to get a credit card instead and work off the debt for the next twenty years.

Dreams are strange. Broken dreams are stranger, but golden ones are harder to let go of. But I have to let go. I have to give in to the Yukon and let the cold winter in. I have to let go of the ghosts that fill me with admiration, let go of the sparkle, the Curse and the fever, let go of the thrill of finding untouched gold older than time itself but as perfect as the day it was created, let go of the adventure of following creeks from the river up into inhospitable mountains that stand like gatekeepers of the Yukon's soul. But above all I have to let go of *Wise Mike*, Pimms and prosperity. It's hard to face the reality of the situation – in this endless remote wilderness which thousands of men have struggled to reach, that has made many men millionaires and which many men have left with riches beyond their capacity to spend, the only way I'm going to get out of here is with Visa!

A lucky chance

Back at the cabin Boris relaxes on the deck right in my way as I stack wood for the winter. Although he refuses to budge, he always looks concerned as I step over him carrying an armful of split wood. Eventually I tap his backside with my boot to let him know that despite his hopes he really is in the way and has to move. He groans and heaves himself on to his short stubby legs, yawns then groans a little more as he walks ten feet and slumps down again in a place I'll have to move him from in ten minutes.

There is a whisper around town that some bench claims in the Gold Fields are about to lapse. As far as I can tell they have been staked since the gold rush and are now owned by a rich American who bought them a few years ago but has not returned to mine them since. If a claim is not mined for a year, it lapses on its birthday and is open for re-staking. This happens all the time, but for it to happen in the heart of the Klondike Gold Fields is extremely rare, because in the last 108 years twenty million ounces of gold with an average price of $600 an ounce has been taken out and everyone knows billions of dollars are still left, so claims can literally be worth millions. It takes time to discover and recover gold and 108 years is no time at all when you're dealing with Klondike gold, 50°C below and the Yukon's whim.

I eventually track down a map of the Gold Fields and am amazed at the number of claims that line the creeks and cover the benches in straight uniform squares. Every last inch of land is staked and has been since late August 1896. This is the kingdom of the Klondike Kings, rugged men who were prospecting the Yukon long before the big strike. They were here first, grubbing about in the dirt looking for gold when they heard of George Carmack's find and rushed to stake the Klondike. Many were on their last legs before they staked on Bonanza or Eldorado, but their claims on the richest creeks in the world made them all extremely rich and turned many into flamboyant legendry characters who threw gold around as if it were candy. When the 40,000 stampeders finally staggered into Dawson they found little land to stake, and witnessed the Klondike Kings strolling into bars and buying a round for the house with wet gold fresh from the sluicebox, or saw them throw their poke on to the poker table and cry: 'The sky's the limit! Raise 'er up as far as you want to go boys, and if the roof's in the way, why, tear it off!'

The map of the Gold Fields shows that the claims rumoured to be lapsed are actually still active so I decide to ask the mining recorder's office to confirm the rumours. The day is cold and the smoke dense in the air as I walk down Front Street in Dawson towards the mining recorder's office. I can't see the surrounding hills or the thin autumn sun that I know is high in the sky. The river looks blue and the air has the tainted smell of burning forests. It could be the middle of June – the forest fire smoke that's coming from Alaska is as thick as it gets in the height of summer.

The mining recorder's office has air conditioning, which, mixed with the smell of warm office equipment, sends a shiver down my spine like a visit from a ghost. The friendly lady behind the desk is only too pleased to help and prints off the latest map of the area I'm interested in. When it's finished curling out of the office-grey machine, she struggles not to crease it as she brings it over to the counter for me to look at. And there they are, in black and white, thirty bench claims lapsed and open for staking – gold bless Americans! The claims are right in the Gold Fields high on a bench overlooking the Klondike River with the famous Bonanza Creek running along their south-west side. I feel my pulse quicken with excitement and the fever burn.

While I'm in the office, several weather-beaten miners in dirt-stained clothes are studying maps quietly and secretively, each one not wanting to give away anything that might tell where he's prospecting. Men come and go, but several ask about two neighbouring claims on Bonanza Creek. I hear familiar names whispered to the clerks who have the well-thumbed map already out on the desk. The men are all asking about the claim owned by a murdered man and the one owned by his former neighbour who shot him in the head with a large calibre rifle last spring. With one man dead and the other sentenced last week to twenty-five years in jail, there are two claims on Bonanza Creek that will definitely lapse some time soon and already a mass of men are preparing to race to stake them at midnight on the date they lapse.

The race to stake lapsed claims has been commonplace in the Klondike ever since the winter of 1896 when the true value of the willow-choked creeks and good-for-nothing moose pasture was being discovered by men getting $800 to the pan even before they had reached the bedrock. Before this a 10-cents pan was considered a good pan. Some old-time prospectors who had staked on Bonanza in August were still skeptical. They had been on many of the big world rushes and many had been worthless so they had left the Klondike to go back to the Forty Mile where they knew gold was in the gravel, without registering their new claims. Under mining law their claims lapsed within sixty days of being staked because they were not registered with the mining recorder, and unbeknown to them their skepticism was losing them millions.

It was on a dark cold night in early November 1896 that one such claim, Sixty Above on Bonanza, was due to lapse. On the claims either side of Sixty Above men had hauled fortunes to the surface all winter long, but Sixty Above was yet un-mined and the date on its claim posts was about to run out. Men desperate to stake rich ground gathered at the claim boundary as midnight neared. The air was brittle, and the squabbles and shouts of the men echoed down the winter-gripped creek. As the clock ticked the tension rose, so a Mountie was posted to keep order amongst the crowd of men all eager to stake the claim and rush to Forty Mile to register.

As the clock ticked slowly towards midnight, less hardy men were beaten back to town by the plunging temperature. With so many men waiting on the claim boundary, the chances of staking first were minimal, so more men dropped out and consoled themselves with watered-down whisky in the warmth of a dance hall in Dawson. But two stuck it out, determined to be millionaires, a Scotsman and a Swede, both desperate and both willing to loose fingers or toes to the brutal night for a chance to stake the claim that could make them rich beyond imagination. Each man had his stakes prepared and ready to hammer into the snow at the witching hour. Finally, on the stroke of midnight, the claim fell open and both men rammed their stakes into the ground before leaping on their dogsleds and racing down Bonanza Creek and out onto the Yukon and heading for Forty Mile nearly 60 miles down river. The men worked their dogs hard as they mushed through the ice fog and dark of the night.

The foggy morning saw them running sporadically behind their teams as frost built up in their beards. Both men needed to get to the mining recorder's office before it shut at five o'clock that evening. They passed and re-passed one other in silent conflict as each tried hard not to think of losing the potential millions he so nearly had in his hands. As the wood smoke of Forty Mile could be smelt in the air and the lights from the cabins seen winking in the dark trees, the Scotsman's dogs began to fail and slowed to a walk. He immediately leapt from his sled and ran towards the settlement. The Swede, whose dogs were also tiring, ran after him until they were neck and neck, running up the bank and into the alleyways of ramshackle log cabins that made up the post. The Swede, who was unfamiliar with the place, dashed for the largest building which was in fact the police officers' mess. The Scotsman let him pass, before dodging right towards the mining recorder's office. Just as the office was closing the Scotsman fell across the threshold and shouted, 'Sixty Above on Bonanza!' A split second later the Swede did the same.

Staking and fortunes

I leave the mining recorder's office full of excitement. Adventure is in the air, time is pressing and a fortune may be at stake. Other people will quickly learn of these claims lapsing if they don't already know. I need to stake them quickly and properly. I need to stake now and I'm going to need help. I go to see Brent, my good friend and neighbour. He's in his yard with his dogs when I drive up to his cabin in the woods. He looks up briefly on my arrival but continues cleaning up the dog pooh.

I feel a bit hesitant and even slightly foolish as I explain about the claims, the need to hurry and the need for secrecy, but as I talk I see a broad smile stretch across Brent's face. He drops his shovel and runs to his shed shouting, 'I'll get the axe!' Moments later we are in my truck and trying to decide where to park near to the Gold Fields that won't draw attention to us.

Smoke is thick in the air but a wind has picked up which might clear it a little. As we hike up the hill out of the Klondike valley and into the Gold Fields we walk through large valley spruce draped in moss and lichen, but the higher we climb, the smaller, twisted and weather-beaten the trees become. We hope no-one has seen us park, and as we hike we listen for the sound of anybody ahead of us in the quiet forests, but all we hear is the slight rustling of the forest canopy as it whispers above us. Blackflies erupt out of the thick spongy moss beneath our feet and cloud around our sweating faces as we cross the tops of gulches that have carried gold for millions of years to the river below. A bleached-white moose skeleton is scattered through the spruce trees, and golden birch leaves float and dance on the light breeze as they leave the trees and fall to the ground. The view behind us is spectacular. It looks out over the Klondike valley. The 'worm castings' or tailing piles, vast rock piles that used to be the riverbed, snake for miles, twisting and turning in the valley and tracking forever the movements of ancient dredges that created them.

The first lapsed claim post takes some finding, and as we walk round in circles looking for the tell-tale squared-off top, we have to be very careful not to trespass on the neighbouring claim – that's one way to get shot. Old mining shafts sunk into the side of the hill loom out of the thick moss like graves, all adding to our excitement. Eventually we find the first claim post, rotting and forgotten and leaning against a birch tree. It must have been here for years. The official metal tag is dull and falling off but is still legible and has the number we are looking for. Excitedly we fell a tree and make another claim post, and wire it to the same birch that has supported the old one. The new one shines with fresh cut wood as we write our names on it:

Dorian Amos. Brent MacDonald
Post 1
Prospecting lease 2 miles
17[b] of August 2005

This officially claims the ground as ours. With that done we move on to the next post two miles up stream on the top of the hill. As we walk along high above the Klondike we move through beautiful golden birch glades and tall stands of mature spruce and into gulches where the trickle of water can be heard below the deep moss. We find the post and again cut a new one and stake the ground as ours. As Brent writes his name on the freshly-cut post I see a glint I his eye, and I know what is fuelling it.

It is late afternoon by the time we get back to the truck and see the time. We have about ten minutes before the mining recorder's office shuts at five and we have to register today to secure the claims. After driving like a seventeen- year-old in his dad's car we arrive at the mining recorder's office at three minutes to five and burst in the door to register our claims. The helpful smiling lady I saw earlier is not smiling at us now. She takes off her coat with a sigh and pulls out the map to process our registration. That is when I see that the freshly-printed map of earlier this morning is now grubby and well handled. It also has pencil marks where the lapsed claims are, so somebody was up there with us, and we are a little nervous until the stamp of approval is clearly on our registration documents and we have paid our $50. When the stamp hits the paper both Brent and I wear huge smiles and shake each other's grubby hands. We are now the proud owners of two miles of gold claims that could potentially hold millions of dollars of perfect Klondike gold.

It's not until we leave the office and are standing in the cooling air outside that I realise the date. It's the 17th of August, the same day George Carmack staked his claim in 1896.

THE DISCOVERY

Boris looks old as he climbs with a groan off the willow seat on the deck to make way for me and a hot cup of tea – he shouldn't be on the furniture anyway. As I sit in the cool morning air, Little Jack comes running out of the cabin and cuddles up to me, hiding from the chill under my jacket. He sniffs the air and says with a smile, 'Smell that, Dad'. I breathe deeply and inhale the crisp autumn morning, and he smiles again and says, 'Isn't it wonderful', just like his mother does most mornings. Uncontrollable love flows out of me to him and I hug him tightly and kiss his forehead which makes him cross, so he skips and dances back into the cabin singing some sort of made-up rhyme. I love that little guy with all my heart.

I agree the Yukon is wonderful. And it is even more wonderful to me because Brent and I went back to our claims and filled a bucket with gravel from a bank to see what was in it. We could not believe our eyes when we got an average of nine flakes of raw Klondike gold to the pan from just one bucket of gravel taken randomly from our two miles of land. At that rate we really could be sitting on millions and millions of dollars of gold. Yes ... the Yukon is wonderful to me again.

A whiskey jack lands on the railing of the deck and searches the woodstove for any scraps left on the grid from last night's moose steaks. I watch the mist rise out of the valley and my thoughts turn to moose hunting. I have time to get the winter's meat now the claims are staked.

I feel relaxed as I plan a moose hunting trip. I might go up the Stewart River for five days or down the McQueston River in *Nugget*. I might even take Jack. I'm happy that I can think about these things now – now that I have the gold. Before we start mining we need to wait for winter to freeze the ground so we can burn shafts safely down to the bedrock, so for now I have time, time to think, time to hunt, and time to be a father.

My search for the Yukon gold has been a long one. For two years I have looked into the dark gravel and bedrock creases for its glitter. For two years I have dragged my family up lonely creeks and through dense forest and over brittle mountains in my search for the Yukon's gold. And in that time the Yukon lost all beauty for me. She has been a hindrance to my search. She has thrown problems and hurdles, ice and snow, fire and flood constantly in my way. Her moods have become unpredictable and harsh. She has literally become ugly and painful to live with and I have struggled and fought with her daily.

But during my search I have discovered the true wilds of the real Yukon. I have gone into that wilderness and been lonely, lost, forgotten and tired, but I have always met someone there, waiting deep in that wilderness, who made me carry on, and it took me a while to realise who it was ... It was the Yukon.

I realise now that the real Yukon, the Yukon I've been struggling with and fighting against, is me and me alone. It's into the wilderness of myself that I went during the search for the Klondike gold, and I met myself there, digging deep into cold gravel on lonely creeks, trying to relate, squashing anguish, fighting failure, surmounting challenges and ultimately discovering. It's me that wanted the gold and it's me that sought it – the Yukon wilderness is not to blame for that. I am the one who was failing, who froze his feet, who got whipped by storms and who threw his shovel in temper. I was the one blinded by the glitter of gold and the promises it made. We didn't need gold. We will never really need gold.

It was me that drove us onto dead men, that put us in danger of predatory bears, chased wolves down mountains, nearly died in turbulent rivers, outran forest fires, but it was the Yukon wilderness and the Klondike that gave us the gold. I climbed lots of mountains in my search, but most were my mountains, I made them high, I made them hard and I had to conquer them as I felt the winds, saw the ghosts and cried in despair... For all of that I'm truly thankful. The Yukon is really my soul and I found myself in the search for gold, but I could not conquer because one can never conquer oneself and should not even try.

The Yukon wilderness, the one with the endless blue mountains, silvery nights and snaking rivers that lies mysteriously above the 60th parallel, is a place, a real place, a place where you come to talk to Elders, run with wolves, dance with the lights, outrun fire, eat moose and lay your ghosts. It is a place to be free to be challenged, a place to get tired, to be lonely. It is also a place to accomplish unthinkable challenges, to fail spectacularly and to make mistakes as frequently as footsteps. It is a place to be happy. It is not necessarily your home, the end of the road, a doorway or a grave. It is a place where you work hard for basics like meat and heat. It's a beautiful place in which to hate, despise, admire and love yourself. Because it is you yourself that you will meet here and finally spend time with, as you fly with ravens, walk with caribou, and dig for gold.

Gold bless all who seek adventure, themselves and the gold... The Curse of the Klondike is waiting... I'm going moose hunting, for tomorrow I dig.

The Beginning...

If you have enjoyed this – then perhaps you
would also enjoy

THE GOOD LIFE

Which tells of Dorian and Bridget's decision to leave the UK
and how they arrived and settled in The Yukon.

Also look out for the next book

THE GOOD LIFE IS BEST

Where you will discover if their new claims produce and take
them to Eldorado (and Wise Mike).

If you want to receive notification of the launch of The Good
Life is Best, then please email thegoodlife@eye-books.com

FACTS ABOUT CANADA'S YUKON TERRITORY

In the Athapaskan language, the word "Yukon" means "the great river" or "big river". At 3,600 kilometres (2,300 miles), the Yukon River is the fourth longest river in North America, the fifth largest in water flow and the last major river on the continent to be explored. The Yukon Territory covers 483,450 square kilometres (186,661 sq. miles). That's larger than the State of California and larger than Belgium, Denmark, Germany and the Netherlands combined.

Caribou	185,000
People	31,881
Black bears	7,000
Birds	(species) 254
Moose	50,000
Mountain sheep	25,000
Grizzly bears	10,000
Fish	(species) 38

The human population of Yukon was higher in 1898 than it is now. Dawson City alone reached a population of over 30,000 at the height of the Klondike Gold Rush. The population of Whitehorse, the current capital of Yukon, was 23,133 in 1993.

A RICH CULTURAL HERITAGE

The Yukon First Nations people include the Southern and Northern Tutchone, Tlingit, Tagish, Kaska, Tanana, Han and Gwitchin people. The Inuvialuit people's traditional hunting grounds include the northern Yukon. The Athapaskan language group includes the Tutchone, Tagish, Kaska, Tanana, Han and Gwitchin people – the largest group of Athapaskans today are the Navajo people in the southwestern United States.

RIBBONS OF HIGHWAY

There are 4,734.8 kilometres (2,942.2 mi.) of highway in the Yukon, including some of the most spectacular and unusual drives in the world. The Dempster Highway, the only public road in Canada to cross the Arctic Circle, is an astonishing drive through Arctic tundra. The Klondike Highway roughly follows the route used by the gold seekers of 1898. The Canol Highway is a fabulous trip through pristine wilderness, past white-water rivers and blue-green lakes.

MOUNTAINS AND MORE MOUNTAINS

The St. Elias Mountains in Kluane National Park are the youngest mountains in Canada and also the highest. There are more than 20 summits over 4,200 metres (14,000 ft.), the largest group of high mountains on the continent and one of the world's largest massifs. The highest of these lofty peaks is Mount Logan, Canada's highest mountain at 5,959 metres (19,551 ft.). And they're still growing – a seismograph in the Visitor Reception Centre at Haines Junction records the hundreds of small tremors that occur every year, pushing the St. Elias Mountains ever skyward.

THE ICE QUEEN

Between the rock massifs of the St. Elias Mountains is one of the world's largest non-polar icefields. Huge valley glaciers fill the gulfs between the peaks; the Hubbard Glacier is 112 kilometres (70 mi.) long and the Lowell Glacier is 72 kilometres (45 mi.) long, and they may be 1.6 kilometres (1 mi.) thick in parts. These glaciers make their own weather, scour away tons of rock every day, dam rivers and create lakes.

GALLOPING GLACIERS

The Steele Glacier in Kluane National Park surged for several months in 1966-67, moving over 1.5 billion tons of ice at a rate of up to 15 metres (50 ft.) per day. Surging valley glaciers are not uncommon in Kluane, where the Lowell Glacier has a history of galloping, blocking the Alsek River and forming a lake. There are more than 2,000 glaciers in Kluane National Park including valley glaciers, hanging glaciers, cirque glaciers and rock glaciers.

UNESCO WORLD HERITAGE SITE
One of the Yukon's great treasures, Kluane National Park, is a designated UNESCO World Heritage Site. It contains the wonders of the St. Elias Mountains and its icefields, glacial lakes, wild rivers and pristine forests. Interpretive trails and exhibitions describe the wonders of one of North America's most awe-inspiring wilderness preserves.

CANADIAN HERITAGE RIVERS
The Alsek and the Thirty-Mile are both Canadian Heritage Rivers, and the Bonnet Plume has been nominated for this special status. The Thirty-Mile rushes from lower Lake Laberge, while the Alsek River courses through Kluane National Park past calving glaciers and awesome mountain scenery. The Bonnet Plume is loved by canoeists from around the world for its challenging white-water and outstanding wilderness setting.

NORTHERN FESTIVALS
The Yukon plays host to many Northern festivals. Visit the Yukon during the Yukon Sourdough Rendezvous, Dawson Discovery Days, Klondike Outhouse Races, Yukon International Storytelling Festival, Yukon Quest Dog Sled Race, Frostbite Music Festival or Dawson City Music Festival. See for yourself what all the fuss is about!

LAND OF THE MIDNIGHT SUN
On 21 June, summer solstice, the sun never sets. You can read a book outdoors all night. The midnight sun makes for long summer days, and wondrous carmine and magenta skyscapes that last for hours, rather than minutes.

THE WORLD'S SMALLEST DESERT

The Carcross Desert is affectionately known as the world's smallest desert. The dry climate and wind conditions have created sand dunes and the vegetation has adapted to the surroundings. This pocket desert is a popular tourist attraction.

RARE MINERALS

More than 30 types of rare phosphate minerals have been discovered in the Blow River area. Many of these minerals are new to science. The exceptionally rare lazulite crystals gave Yukon its official gemstone. Samples of these minerals are on display in Whitehorse.

THE BLUE FISH CAVES

The Blue Fish Caves on the Bluefish River in the northern Yukon contain the earliest evidence of human habitation in North America. Some experts believe humans have lived in this region for more than 14,000 years.

SOURDOUGHS AND CHEECHAKOS

Sourdough (a fermenting mixture of flour, water, and a pinch of sugar and rice) hung in a kettle over the wood stove of many Yukoners. It was used as a starter to make delicious sourdough bread. "Sourdough" became the word used to describe a Yukon old-timer. A Cheechako, on the other hand, is a "greenhorn" – or newcomer – to the Yukon. There's only one way for a cheechako to become a sourdough: he or she must watch the river freeze in the fall and break into grinding pieces in the spring. The term "sourdough" was immortalized in Robert Service's first collection of verse, "Songs of the Sourdough".

SNOW IN SUMMER?

Not likely. The Yukon has warm, sunny summers with average temperatures in July of 14°C to 16°C (57°F to 60°F), and highs that can reach 35°C (95°F). The average temperature in January is between -18°C and -25°C (0°F and -15°F), though lows can reach -55°C (-58°F). The Yukon's climate is semi-arid, so snow and rainfall are light; on average there's just 26.8 centimetres (10.5 in.) of precipitation a year in Whitehorse, the capital.

About Eye Books

Eye Books is a dynamic, young publishing company that likes to break the rules. Our independence allows us to publish books which challenge the way people see things. It also means that we can offer new authors a platform from which they can shine their light and encourage others to do the same.

Please visit www.eye-books.com for further information.

Eye Club Membership

Each month, we receive hundreds of enquiries from people who have read our books, discovered our website or entered our competitions. All these people have certain things in common: a desire to achieve, to extend the boundaries of everyday life and to learn from others' experiences.

Eye Books has, therefore, set up a club to unite these like-minded people. It is a community where members can exchange ideas, contact authors, discuss travel, both future and past, as well as receive information and offers from Eye Books.

Membership is free.

Benefits of the Eye Club

As a member of the Eye Club:

• You are offered the invaluable opportunity to contact our authors directly.
• You will receive a regular newsletter, information on new book releases and company developments as well as discounts on new and past titles.
• You can attend special member events such as book launches, author talks and signings.
• Receive discounts on a variety of travel-related products and services from Eye Books' partners.
• You can enjoy entry into Eye Books competitions including the ever popular Heaven and Hell series and our monthly book competition.

To register your membership, simply visit our website and register on our club pages: www.eye-books.com.

2006 Titles

Fateful Beauty – the story of Frances Coke 1602-1642 – Natalie Hodgson

Fateful Beauty is the true story of a young woman who, at the age of fifteen, was forced to marry a mentally unstable man by her ambitious father, the Lord Chancellor, Sir Edward Coke, auther of the Petition of Rights. The book is well researched and gives a vivid picture of the late sixteenth and early seventeenth centuries - political intrigue, the Elizabethan and Stuart courts, civil war, domestic life and the place of women in society.

ISBN 1 903070 406. Price £12.99.

On the Wall with Hadrian – Bob Bibby

The newly opened Hadrian's Wall path, 84 miles (135km) long, stretching from coast to coast in the north of England, inspired travel writer Bob Bibby to don his boots and explore its Roman origins. The book describes Hadrian, his period and the life of his soldiers and provides an up-to-date guide on where to stay, eat and drink along the Path.

ISBN 978 1 903070 499. Price £9.99.

Siberian Dreams – Andy Home

Journalist, Andy Home realised that without the Siberian city of Norislk and its inhabitants, the lives of Westerners would have to change. He visits this former Prison Camp now mining city in the Artic Circle to find out what life is like for the 200,000 people living in sub-zero temperatures in Russia's most polluted city.

ISBN 978 1 903070 512. Price £9.99.

Changing the World. One Step at the time – Michael Meegan

Many people say they want to make a difference but don't know how. This book offers examples of real people making real differences. It reminds us to see joy and love in every moment of every day, and that making a difference is something everyone can do.

ISBN 978 1 903070 444. Price £9.99

Prickly Pears of Palestine – Hilda Reilly

The Palestinian/Israeli conflict is one of the most widely reported and long standing struggles in the world yet misunderstood by many. Author Hilda Reilly spent time living and working in the region to put some human flesh on these bare stereotypical bones and try and make the situation comprehensible for the bewildered news consumer.

ISBN 978 1 903070 529. Price £9.99.

Also by Eye Books

Zohra's Ladder – Pamela Windo
A wondrous collection of stories of Moroccan life that offer a privileged immersion into a world of deep sensuality. ISBN 1 903070 406. Price £9.99.

Great Sects – Adam Hume Kelly
Essential insights into sects for the intellectually curious – from Kabbalah to Dreamtime, Druidry to Opus Dei. ISBN: 1903070 473. Price £9.99.

Blood Sweat & Charity – Nick Stanhope
The guide to charity challenges. ISBN: 1 903070 414. Price £12.99.

Death – The Great Mystery of Life – Herbie Brennan
A compulsive study, its effect is strangely liberating and life enhancing.
ISBN: 1 903070 422. Price £9.99.

Riding the Outlaw Trail – Simon Casson
An equine expedition retracing the footsteps of those legendary real-life bandits, Butch Cassidy and the Sundance Kid. ISBN: 1 903070 228. Price £9.99.

Green Oranges on Lion Mountain – Emily Joy
A VSO posting in Sierra Leone where adventure and romance were on the agenda; rebel forces and threat of civil war were not. ISBN: 1 903070 295. Price £9.99.

Desert Governess – Phyllis Ellis
A former Benny Hill Show actress becomes a governess to the Saudi Arabian Royal Family.
ISBN: 1 903070 015. Price £9.99.

Last of the Nomads – W. J. Peasley
The story of the last of the desert nomads to live permanently in the traditional way in Western Australia.
ISBN: 1 903070 325. Price £9.99.

All Will Be Well – Michael Meegan
A book about how love and compassion when given out to others can lead to contentment.
ISBN: 1 903070 279. Price £9.99.

First Contact – Mark Anstice
A 21st-century discovery of cannibals.
Comes with (free) DVD which won the Banff Film Festival.
ISBN: 1 903070 260. Price £9.99.

Further Travellers' Tales From Heaven and Hell – Various
This is the third book in the series of real travellers tales.
ISBN: 1 903070 112. Price £9.99.

Special Offa – Bob Bibby
A walk along Offa's Dyke.
ISBN: 1 903070 287. Price £9.99.

The Good Life – Dorian Amos
A move from the UK to start a new life in the wilderness of The Yukon.
ISBN: 1 903070 309. Price £9.99.

Baghdad Business School – Heyrick Bond Gunning
The realities of a business start-up in a war zone.
ISBN: 1 903070 333. Price £9.99.

The Accidental Optimist's Guide to Life – Emily Joy
Having just returned from Sierra Leone, a busy GP with a growing family ponders the meaning of life.
ISBN: 1 903070 430. Price £9.99.

The Con Artist Handbook – Joel Levy
Get wise as this blows the lid on the secrets of the successful con artist and his con games.
ISBN: 1 903070 341. Price £9.99.

The Forensics Handbook – Pete Moore
The most up-to-date log of forensic techniques available.
ISBN: 1 903070 35X. Price £9.99.

My Journey With A Remarkable Tree – Ken Finn
A journey following an illegally logged tree from a spirit forest to the furniture corner of a garden centre.
ISBN: 1 903070 384. Price £9.99.

Seeking Sanctuary – Hilda Reilly
Western Muslim converts living in Sudan.
ISBN: 1 903070 392. Price £9.99.

Lost Lands Forgotten Stories – Alexandra Pratt
The retracing of an astonishing 600 mile river journey in 1905 in 2005.
ISBN: 1 903070 368. Price £9.99.

Jasmine and Arnica – Nicola Naylor
A blind woman's journey around India.
ISBN: 1 903070 171. Price £9.99.

Touching Tibet – Niema Ash
A journey into the heart of this intriguing forbidden land.
ISBN: 1 903070 18X. Price £9.99.

Behind the Veil – Lydia Laube
A shocking account of a nurse's Arabian nightmare.
ISBN: 1 903070 198. Price £9.99.

Walking Away – Charlotte Metcalf
A well-known film maker's African journal.
ISBN: 1 903070 201. Price £9.99.

Travels in Outback Australia – Andrew Stevenson
In search of the original Australians – the Aboriginal People.
ISBN: 1 903070 147. Price £9.99.

The European Job – Jonathan Booth
10,000 miles around Europe in a 25-year-old classic car.
ISBN: 1 903070 252. Price £9.99.

Around the World with 1000 Birds – Russell Boyman
An extraordinary answer to a mid-life crisis.
ISBN: 1 903070 163. Price £9.99.

Cry from the Highest Mountain – Tess Burrows
A climb to the point furthest from the centre of the earth.
ISBN: 1 903070 120. Price £9.99.

Dancing with Sabrina – Bob Bibby
A journey along the River Severn from source to sea.
ISBN: 1 903070 244. Price £9.99.

Grey Paes and Bacon – Bob Bibby
A journey around the canals of the Black Country.
ISBN: 1 903070 066. Price £7.99.

Jungle Janes – Peter Burden
Twelve middle-aged women take on the Jungle. As seen on Channel 4.
ISBN: 1 903070 058. Price £7.99.

Travels with my Daughter – Niema Ash
Forget convention, follow your instincts.
ISBN: 1 903070 04X. Price £7.99.

Riding with Ghosts – Gwen Maka
One woman's solo cycle ride from Seattle to Mexico.
ISBN: 1 903070 007. Price £7.99.

Riding with Ghosts: South of the Border – Gwen Maka
The second part of Gwen's epic cycle trip through the
Americas.
ISBN: 1 903070 090. Price £7.99.

Triumph Round the World – Robbie Marshall
He gave up his world for the freedom of the road.
ISBN: 1 903070 082. Price £7.99.

Fever Trees of Borneo – Mark Eveleigh
A daring expedition through uncharted jungle.
ISBN: 0 953057 569. Price £7.99.

Discovery Road – Tim Garrett and Andy Brown
Their mission was to mountain bike around the world.
ISBN: 0 953057 534. Price £7.99.

Frigid Women – Sue and Victoria Riches
The first all-female expedition to the North Pole.
ISBN: 0 953057 52 6. Price £7.99.

Jungle Beat – Roy Follows
Fighting terrorists in Malaya.
ISBN: 0 953057 577. Price £7.99.

Slow Winter – Alex Hickman
A personal quest against the backdrop of the war-torn
Balkans.
ISBN: 0 953057 585. Price £7.99.

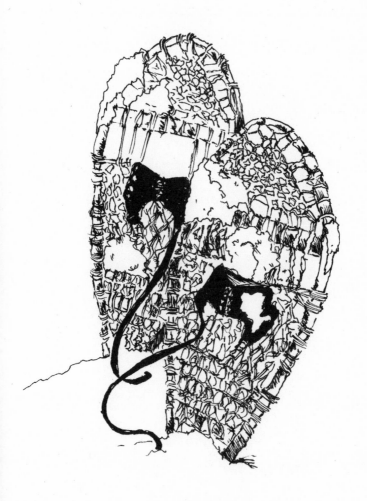